GOOGLE PIXEL & 9 PRO X GUIDE

Detailed Manual with Comprehensive Illustrations on How to Setup and Use Pixel 9 series (Android 14 Manual) with Tips & Tricks for Beginners and Senior

SCOTT WHETZEL

All rights reserved.

Copyright (C) 2024 Scott Wetzel

No section of this book may be duplicated or used in any way without the Publisher's/writer's express consent.

Table of Contents

Introduction 1

   Summary of Google pixel 9, Pixel 9 Pro & Pixel 9 Pro XL features 3

Physical characteristics of your gadget pixel 9 series .. 4

CHAPTER 1 6

Switch your gadget on 6

   Restart or turn off your Google Pixel 9 or Pixel 9 Pro device 7

      Toggle your gadget off via notification shade 7

   Utilize a button to toggle off the power 9

      Use Google Assistant to toggle off your gadget 9

   Reconfigure the power button in settings 10

CHAPTER 2 12

Setup (Configure) your new Device 12

CHAPTER 3 17

Charging your gadget 17

   How to charge your Pixel 9 pro 17

   Activating Fast Charging 18

   Wireless charging 20

   Activating Wireless Charging on the Pixel 9 pro ... 20

   Battery Adaptive and Charging 21

CHAPTER 4 23

Device Security and safety 23

   Setting up Face Unlock 23

How to disable Face Unlock on Pixel 9 and Pixel 9 pro 27

Fingerprint Setup.. 29

    Add a Fingerprint: Steps 29

    If the application lacks fingerprint protection 31

Setting up your gadget smart lock 32

Secure your phone using a pattern and pin 33

    Settings for the screen lock and pattern 33

CHAPTER 5 41

SIM AND e-SIM 41

Acquire a SIM card and insert it into your Pixel phone 41

Inserting a SIM card into your gadget 43

How to utilize a Google Pixel phone with two SIM cards 44

    Add a second SIM card & eSIM 44

    Include a second SIM card 45

Switch SIMs when making calls 45

Turn a SIM off momentarily 46

CHAPTER 6 47

Motion & Gestures 47

Access and modify Quick Settings and notifications 47

Use extra applications 48

Activate/deactivate gestures 48

Access and modify navigation bar settings 50

Use motions gestures for the full-screen 51

Utilize Quick Tap 54

Utilise flip to mute 54

CHAPTER 7 56

Internet and Cellular Info 56

Check your network connection's strength 56

Accessing your cellular data..................................... 57

Activate or deactivate mobile data 58

Turn on or off international data 59

Toggle on or off mobile data quickly 60

Browsing the Internet (web)................................... 62

Accessing the major Browser 62

Go to website 62

Bookmark website 63

Access/open/close browser tabs 64

Accessing your browser setup 65

WiFi/hotspot settings &usage 66

Make use of WiFi... 66

Join a wireless network (wifi) 66

Forget a Network service 67

Connecting to a secret network........................... 68

Mobile (portable) Hotspot 69

Activate/deactivate mobile hotspot 69

Set up the Mobile Hotspot settings.......................71
CHAPTER 8 73
Connectivity..73
    Bluetooth 73
        Switch Bluetooth On & off Using the Settings app
       73
        Switch Bluetooth on or off via quick settings.......73
    Utilize hotspot tethering in sharing connection.....74
        Use Bluetooth to tether 74
        Tethering via USB cable 74
        Transfer files via your device................................75
CHAPTER 9 76
Live Translate 76
    Turn on Live Translation 76
    Using Live Translation on Text Messages 77
    Translate using the camera....................................77
        Translate a discussion into a foreign language using Google Assistant 78
        Use Live Captioning when watching media in any language..78
CHAPTER 10 79
Multitask with your device.......................................79
    Using split-screen modes.......................................79
        What does split-screen mode mean 79
        Open two applications at once 79

Using an app to launch in a pop-up window 80
Accessing your device's split screen 81
Modify the window's size 83
Leave the Split Screen 84
Using Picture-in-Picture 85

CHAPTER 11 87

Photos and Videos 87
Accessing and Archiving Your Photos and Videos . 87
Camera and Video Presets 87
Accessing camera settings on your gadget 87
Adjust or modify your photo's size 88
On/Off the flash switch 89
Place a timer 89
Access the camera and microphone for editing .. 90
Snapping a screenshot 91
Snap a screenshot 91
Editing or sharing screenshots instantly 91
Access and use screen recording 92
Start recording 92
End recording 93
Transfer your videos and photos 94
Media transfer to or via a PC 94
Transferring files to or via Macs 95
Advanced Photos & Videos 97

Access the camera's modes 97
Customize photo and video settings 97
Activate or deactivate the shutter sound 98
Crop a picture 98
Utilize filters 99
Using a magic eraser 99
Utilize Photo Un-blur 101
Utilize Night Vision 102
Utilize the Motion mode 102
Use photo effects 103
Create a video or take pictures 104
Take a picture 104
Swapping between the front-facing and rear-facing cameras 104
Adjust the camera's focus 105
Zoom in and out 105
Activate the Macro mode 106
Access Night Sight and utilize it 107
Use and access Picture Sphere 108
Use and access Panorama 108
Access and utilize Google Lens 109
Record a Video 110
Recording or Making a video 110
Stop, pause, and resume a recording 111

Snap a still picture while in video mode............111
Utilize Slow Motion 112
Utilize Time Lapse..113
Super-res Zoom 114
Cinematic Mode...114
Cinematic Pan..115
Active Stabilization 117
Action Pan...119
Long exposure 120
Astrophotography 122
Setting Macro mode 124
Enhancing Speech 125

CHAPTER 12 128
Game mode..128
Turn on Game Mode 128
Use DND Mode to access the game's dashboard ..131
Access the Game Dashboard through the Google Page 132
Change to English-only 133

CHAPTER 13..135
How to Set Up contactless payment (NFC) on a Google Pixel 9 135
Activating NFC on your gadget 135
Through the use of the notification center 135
Utilizing the device's settings 136

Setting up NFC 137

CHAPTER 14 141

Emergency health and safety measures 141

    How temperature is been measured 141

        How to utilize the temperature-checking app Thermometer 141

    Activate the Snore and Cough Detection 144

    Enable bedtime mode 145

    Activate or deactivate earthquake alerts 146

CHAPTER 15 147

Car crash detection 147

    Set up car crashing detection 147

    Making use of your car crash detection 148

    Activate the car crash detection feature with emergency sharing 149

CHAPTER 16 150

Emergency/sos 150

    Activate and configure Emergency SOS 150

        Select how to begin Emergency SOS 153

        Switch off the emergency SOS 153

        Utilize Emergency SOS to record video, notify contacts, and make an assistance request 154

        Record video in an emergency 154

        Activate or deactivate Emergency Location Service 155

Share and provide your emergency contacts with your location..................155

Quit sharing emergency information 156

CHAPTER 18 157

How to do a factory reset and enter safe mode........157

Safe Mode 157

Leave Safe Mode......................158

Reset Factory settings 158

Reset the phone if it is off or unresponsive.......158

CHAPTER 19 160

Common problems and issues 160

Poor or easily drained battery life 160

Sluggish or laggy user interface 162

Problems with your gadget's camera 163

Your gadget shutting down unexpectedly 164

Stuck or frozen Google Pixel 9 pro screen 165

Slow App Opening....................166

Apps and Games Crash Suddenly or Unexpectedly 167

Bluetooth won't connect.................167

Display broken & touch not functioning 168

WiFi Connection Issue or Limited WiFi Range....169

Mobile data or cellular network issues 170

Applications from the Play Store won't download 170

Problem with the fingerprint scanner 171
Your gadget heating issue 172
BONUS TIPS 174
Whats New in the Google Pixel 9 series 174
Screenshot app 174
Pixel-Studio 174
An improved weather app 174
Magic Editor's Reimagine feature makes editing simpler 175
Using a circle to search updated features 175
Deactivate the circle to search 176
INDEX 177

Introduction

The newest pixel phones include cutting-edge cameras, enhanced performance, practical AI features, and much more. To deliver you the best of Pixel, they are all powered by a brand-new Google Tensor G4 processor.

The Pixel 9 series feature a stylish new design that highlights the camera by evolving a recognizable camera bar. In addition to being beautifully crafted, the design feels nice in the hand. They also have updated finishes, giving off a more premium vibe with polished metal sides and a smooth matte glass back.

The Pixel 9 Pro and Pixel 9 Pro XL have identical specifications and features, except display size, charging speed, and power.

A new unique silicon, called Tensor G4, powers the Pixel 9 phones (series) having The most efficient chip & created to enhance common use cases, such as online surfing and quicker app opening.

Designed with Google DeepMind, Tensor G4 is optimized to execute the most sophisticated artificial intelligence models. It will be the first software to support Gemini Nano with Multimodality, which makes text, photos, and music understandable on your phone.

This manual explains the features, setups and settings ranging from the basics to the most complex features on your new gadget for both newbie or as a senior

Summary of Google pixel 9, Pixel 9 Pro & Pixel 9 Pro XL features

S/N	Features	Pixel 9 pro	Pixel 9 pro XL	Pixel 9
1	Screen size	6.3	6.8	6.3
2	Telephoto lens	48 MP	48 MP	Non
3	Rear video	8K	8K	4K
4	Performance	G4 Tensor chip	G4 Tensor chip	G4 Tensor chip
5	RAM	16 GB	16 GB	12 GB
6	Front camera	42 MP	42 MP	10.5 MP
7	Display	Super Actua	Super Actua	Actua
8	Rear camera	50 MP wide 48 MP ultrawide	50 MP wide 48 MP ultrawide	50 MP wide 48 MP ultrawide

Physical characteristics of your gadget pixel 9 series

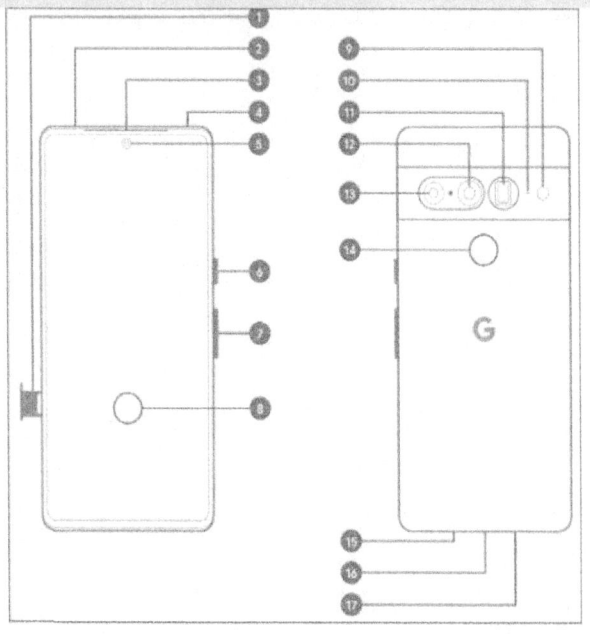

1. SIM card tray
2. Top Microphone
3. Top speaker
4. mmWave antenna cover
5. Front-facing camera
6. Power button
7. Volume up/down button
8. Fingerprint sensor
9. LED flash

10. Rear-facing microphone
11. 5x telephoto lens
12. Ultrawide-lens camera
13. Rear-facing camera
14. NFC
15. Lower mic or speaker
16. USB-C hole
17. Lower MIC

The first thing to do once you purchase or acquire your new pixel gadget is to toggle it on to check out your device. CHAPTER one explains the basics of how you can get your device started as a newbie or as a senior

CHAPTER 1

Switch your gadget on

- Click Hold down the Power button.
- Pause for a while to see a logo exhibited on the screen
- Once the logo pops up, let go of the knob (button).

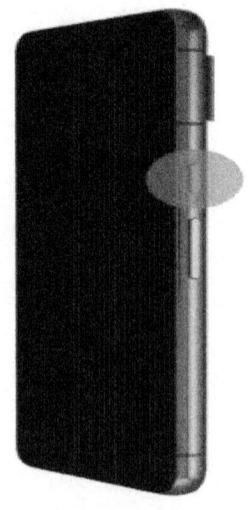

Go to setup your gadget in **CHAPTER 2** if it is the first time you're turning your gadget on to set your device passphrase or lock to get a passphrase option when toggling it on

Restart or turn off your Google Pixel 9 or Pixel 9 Pro device

Here, we'll go through different techniques you may use to switch off your Google Pixel 9 and Pixel 9 Pro.

Toggle your gadget off via notification shade

1. To be able to utilize notification (shade), slide downward via the upper section of your display screen

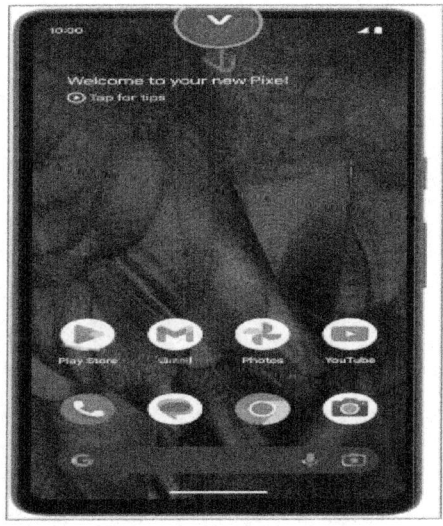

2. To get the fast settings, swipe down one more and let it expand to full-screen
3. A power button should then be visible in the lower right corner

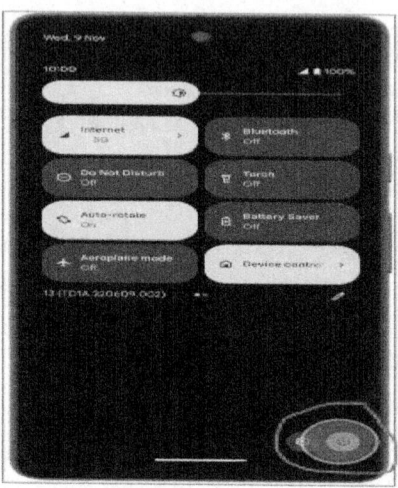

4. Select whether to reset your phone or turn it off by clicking that option.

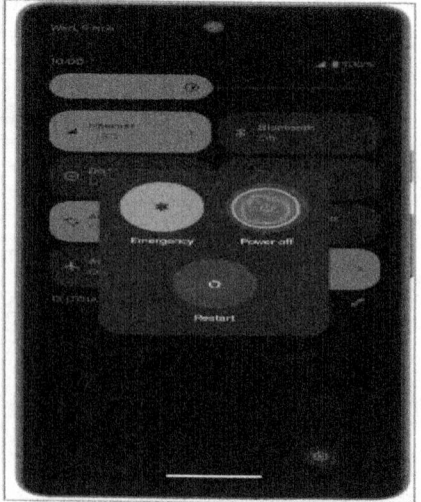

Utilize a button to toggle off the power

To switch off your gadget via the buttons:

1. Hold down the volume up the knob, concurrently & touch down the little power knob
2. pause to Allow the power menu to appear
3. Select Restart or Power Off to restart.

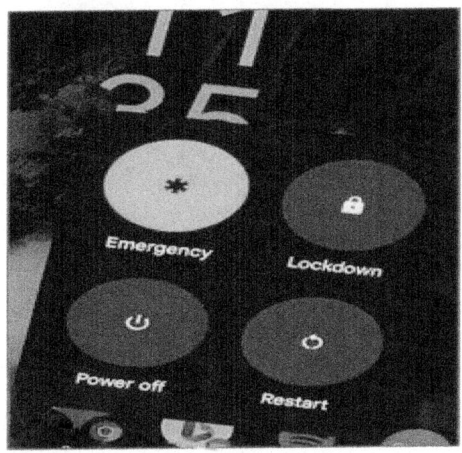

Use Google Assistant to toggle off your gadget

One of the many things you can do with Google's voice assistant is switch off your phone. Several methods exist for doing this:

1. Touch and hold down the control knob to turn on Google Assistant, or speak "Google" to turn it off.
2. If Google is listening, say "turn off" or "restart my phone" to shut off or restart the device.

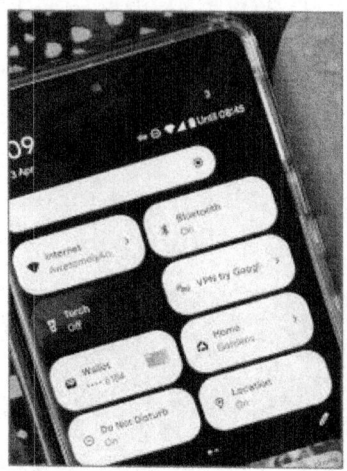

Reconfigure the power button in settings

It is possible to customize a variety of gestures and actions under the system settings. One of them is to change the power button's settings so that the power is truly turned off.

Trail the subsequent phases to complete this:

1. Open up the system settings
2. In the settings menu, scroll downward until you see **the system** at the bottom
3. To navigate the various gestures setups, **Touch Gestures**

4. Locate **press & hold the power button** by scrolling down.
5. Change it to **the power menu**

CHAPTER 2

Setup (Configure) your new Device

Once you have toggled your device on, the next salient thing to do is to configure your gadget. Follow through as we explain every set-up one after the other

Ensure a 5G SIM is inserted into the device before turning it on.

1. If the device is off, hold down the Power button while waiting for the Google logo to display before letting go.
2. Pick the suitable language via the **"Welcome to your Pixel"** display screen, and now hit on**"Get started."**

3. Hit on Continue via the "Phone activation" display screen.
4. input the account password if asked, and now trail abide by the on-display screen guidelines
5. Make sure the old phone is turned off before activating the new one.
6. Choose a network from the "Connect to Wi-Fi" menu, then input the password.
7. If you select "Skip," you can add a Wi-Fi network after the installation is finished.
8. Select and pick any of the subsequent preferences via the "Copy apps & info/data" display:
    - Next
    - Do not copy

9. Input Google Mail info in the "log in" rectangular box, & now hit **"Next."** You will be able to include your Google account when setup is concluded if you hit**"Skip."**
10. Choose the desired selections from the "Google Services" screen, then hit Accept.
11. Select "Not now" or "Turn on" when the "Back up your mobile device with Google One" screen appears
12. Choose the desired option from the "Verizon Services" menu, then touch "I accept." From the "Limited Warranty" page, select Next to proceed.
13. Tap I accept on the "Additional legal conditions" page to proceed.
14. Input a password digit on the "input a password" display, then hit next.

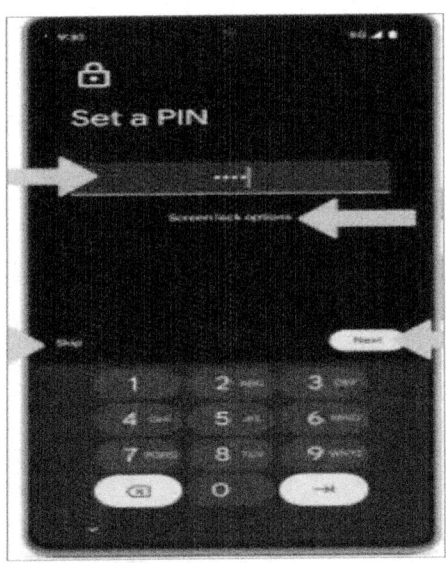

15. Tap Screen lock options to configure a pattern or password.
16. If you select "Skip," setup will be finished before you can set up a screen lock, fingerprint reader, or facial recognition.
17. From the "Continue setup?" page, click the Continue icon to conclude the configuration& personalization of your gadget
18. **Hit on Leave** to be able to start reminders later
19. Read the information on the "Talk to Google hands-free" screen, then press **"I accept"** to activate "Hey Google."
20. Once the activation process is complete, tap Skip to install Google Assistant.
21. Tap **"I accept"** or **"Skip"** from the "Access your assistant without unlocking your phone" screen to allow Assistant on the lock screen.

22. Set up more things from the "Anything else" screen or select "No thanks."
23. Select the options "Yes, I'm in" or "No thanks" from the "Get more tips & techniques" page.
24. Tap Try it on the "Swipe to navigate your phone" screen.
25. Tap Skip if you don't want to learn how to use gestures to switch between apps, go Home, and go back.
26. To navigate to the Home display screen via the "All set!" "display screen, slide up via the bottom of your device.

CHAPTER 3

Charging your gadget

After you have finished setting up your gadget, it is pertinent to first charge up your device to full so that your device can have a long-lasting battery life

To achieve this, adhere to the guidelines listed below.

How to charge your Pixel 9 pro

1. Use the original charger or the one that came with your gadget
2. Connect to a Stable Power Source
3. Connect your gadget charger to a reliable power supply and plug the other end into your device itself
    - To make sure your Google Pixel 9 pro smartphone has a steady power source, use a wall outlet or an approved charging port.

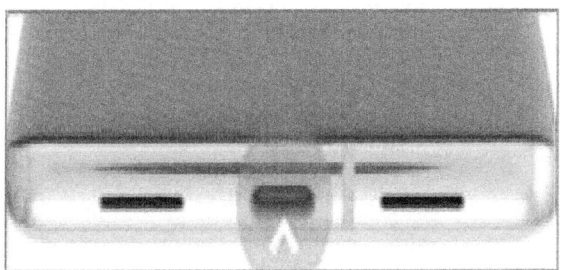

Activating Fast Charging

Activating the feature in the settings

1. Navigate to Settings

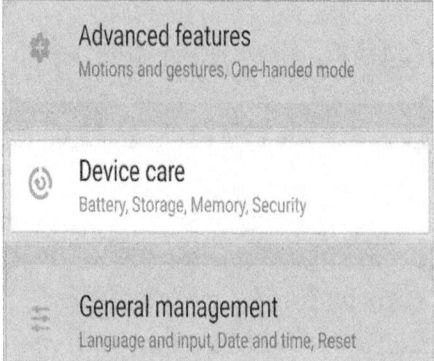

2. Hit on Device care

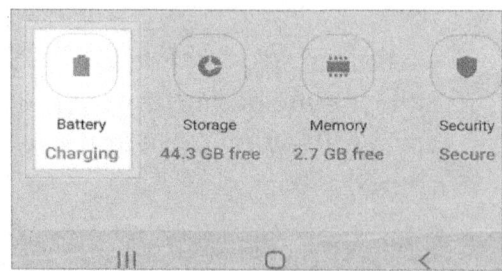

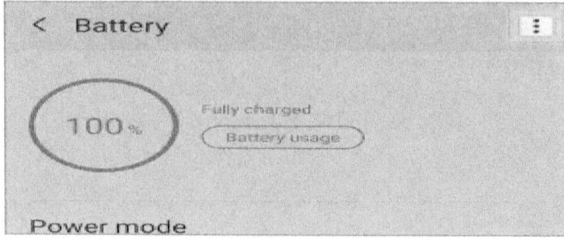

3. Hit on Battery
4. Hit on Settings

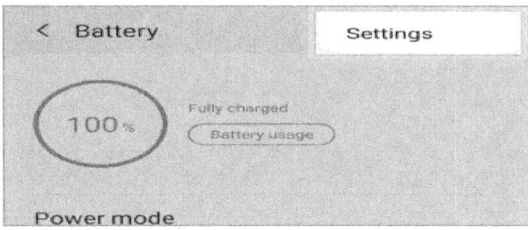

5. Toggle switch: Set to the "On" position.

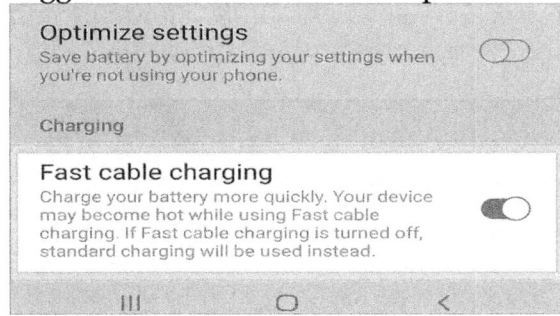

Wireless charging

Activating Wireless Charging on the Pixel 9 pro

1. **Verify that wireless charging is supported.** Check to see whether yourPixel 9 pro has wireless charging capability. Although the Pixel 9 pro has built-in wireless charging, it's a good idea to verify.
2. **Purchase a wireless charger.** You'll need a wireless charger to enable wireless charging on your Pixel 9 pro. There are several choices, including charging stands and pads.
3. Choose the one that best meets your requirements and budget.
4. **Connect the wireless charger.** Utilize the supplied cable to attach the wireless charger to a power source. Make sure that the charger is correctly connected & switched on.
5. **Place your Pixel 9 pro on the chargerto complete.** Make sure your Pixel 9 pro is correctly aligned with the charger's specified charging area before setting it down on the wireless charger. To make a connection, you might need to gently modify your posture
6. **Verify the charging status**. A charging indication should show up on the screen as soon as your Pixel 9 pro is connected to the charger. On the lock screen or in the

notification panel, you may also check the status.
7. Take advantage of wireless charging's ease. You may now enjoy the comfort of charging your device without the inconvenience of wires thanks to the wireless charging feature that has been activated on your Pixel 9 pro.

Battery Adaptive and Charging

1. Start your Pixel 9 pro's Settings app. Navigate to your gadget's battery section

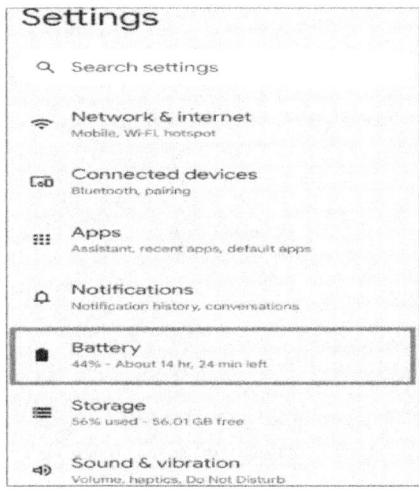

2. Go to Adaptive preferences

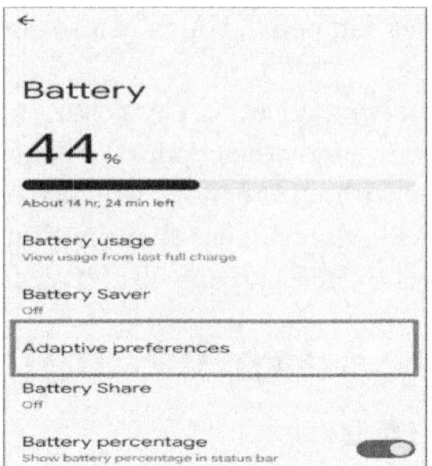

3. Turn on the toggles next to Adaptive Charging and Adaptive Battery in step three.

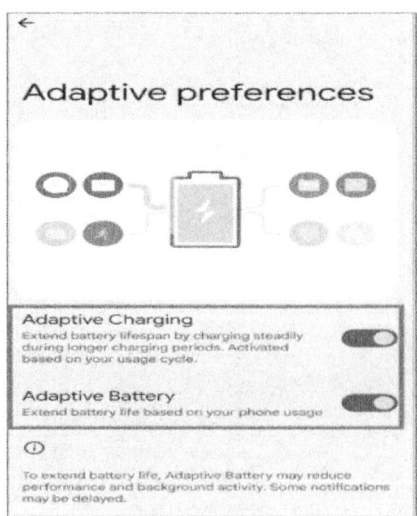

CHAPTER 4

Device Security and safety

Once your gadget is fully charged and configured, you will have to set up security on your phone to avoid uninvited guest access.

Below, we will run through a brief on how you can go about setting up different locks, such as facial, fingerprint, password or pin code, patterns, and smart unlock

Setting up Face Unlock

1. Access Settings

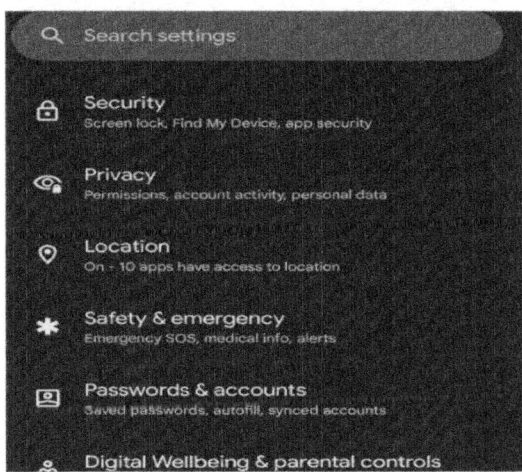

2. Select Security

3. Press Fingerprint and Face Unlock

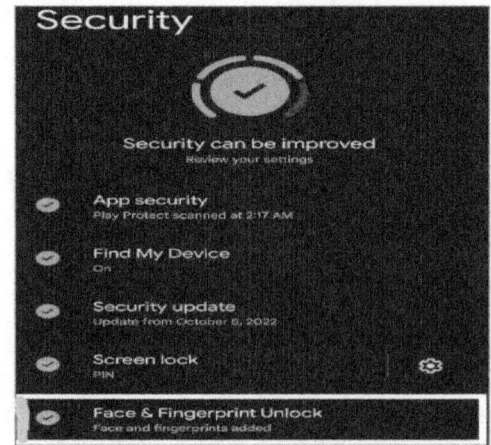

4. Hit on Face Unlock and then

5. Click Set up Face Unlock

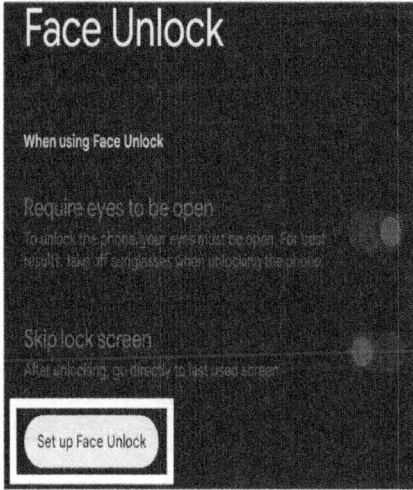

6. Position your head in the middle of the loop icon.
7. When the procedure is finished, tap the Done button.

How to disable Face Unlock on Pixel 9 and Pixel 9 pro

1. Slide downward twice via the upper of the display screen, or once with two fingers, to launch the settings on your gadget
2. Click Security on the lower right
3. Select Fingerprint & Face Unlock

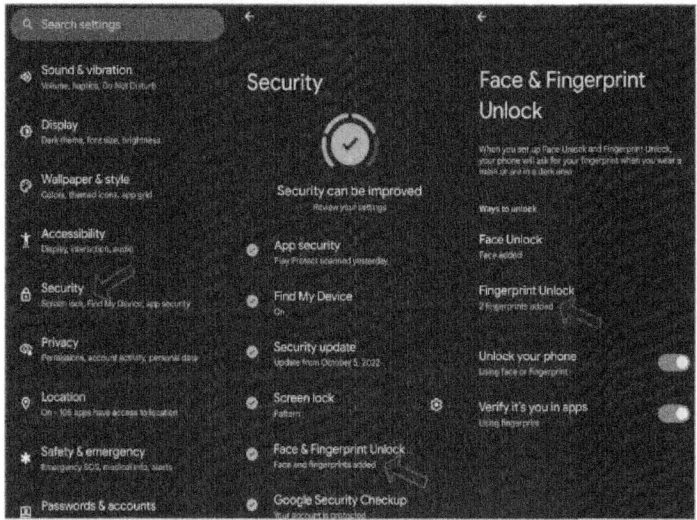

4. Choose Face Unlock
5. Type in your security pattern or PIN
6. Select Delete face model
7. Select Delete.

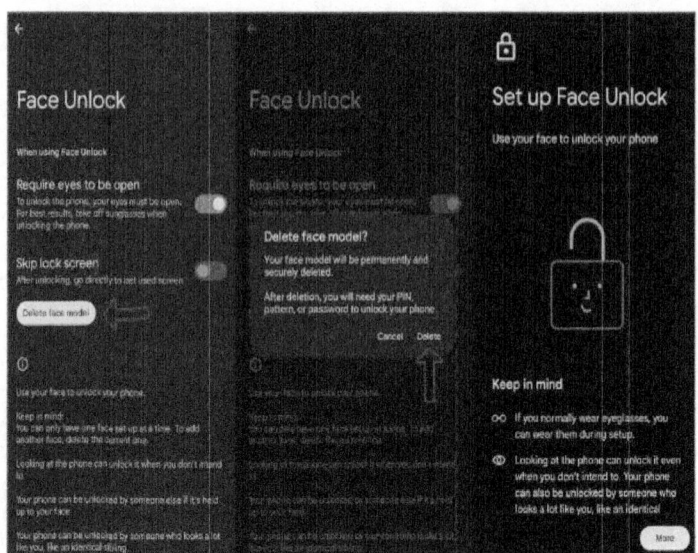

After completing those procedures, your phone will no longer require your face to unlock it. Follow the following instructions to re-enable the function; however, in Step 6, you will be presented with the setup procedure

Fingerprint Setup

Add a Fingerprint: Steps

No matter what information you wish to keep private on the Google Pixel 9 pro, you must first register the main fingerprint. Normally, you will be asked to do this after turning on the device for the first time, but if you forgot, you may add security after the fact:

1. Proceed to your phone's settings.
2. Go to the "Lock screen and fingerprints" area (occasionally this part is named "Biometrics and security") to find the item you're searching for

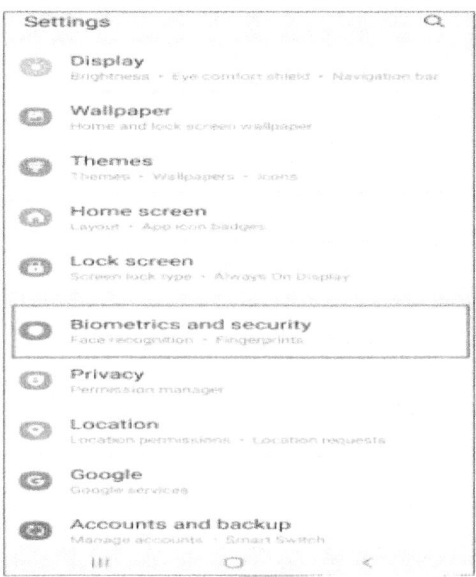

3. Choosing "Fingerprints"

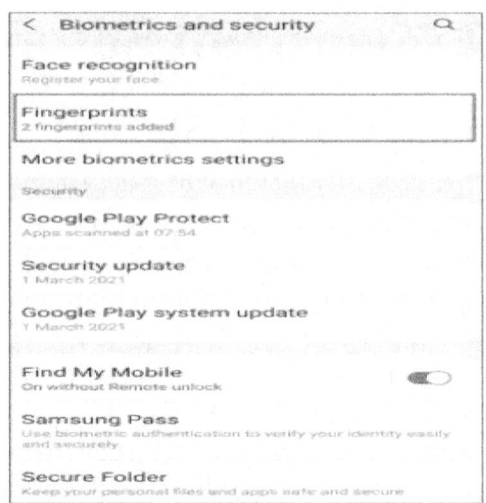

4. Press "Add fingerprint" and then adhere to the directions that display.

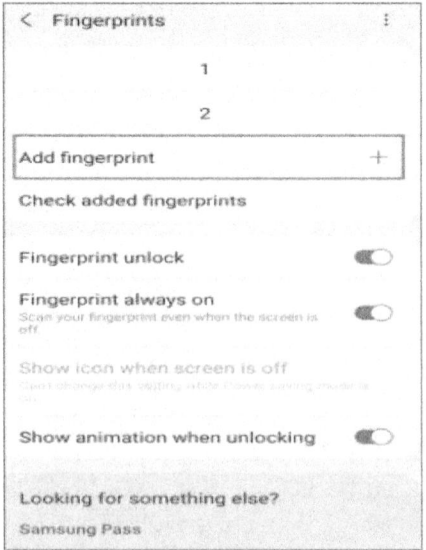

If the application lacks fingerprint protection,

If the application lacks fingerprint protection

1. Proceed to your phone's settings.
2. In the menu, choose "Application lock" (the name may vary depending on the firmware version)
3. Examine the applications on which you wish to impose protection
4. Verify in the settings that the fingerprint scanner is being used.

An attacker will now be prevented from launching even the most innocent program since the Google Pixel 9 pro will ask them for their fingerprint.

Setting up your gadget smart lock

When your phone is in a certain trusted environment, Smart Lock is a set of choices that keep it unlocked and free from any authentication needs.

Do the following:

1. Go back to your system settings and choose Security again, but this time select "More security settings."
2. Your finger should be pressed down into the "Smart Lock" line.
3. When asked, enter your PIN, password, or pattern. After that, check over the various Smart Lock choices and consider which could make the most sense for you.

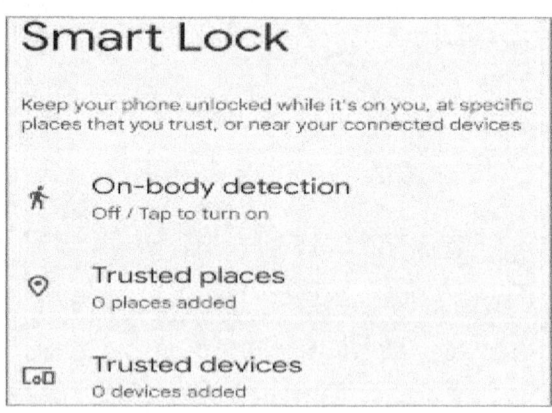

Secure your phone using a pattern and pin

Settings for the screen lock and pattern

1. Before you begin
    - Begin with the subsequent stage if you intend to modify the SIM password.
    - Go straight to step 12 if you want to configure a lock screen on your phone.
    - Before you begin the guide, make sure you have your Public SIM PIN.
2. Slide upward

3. Navigate to and choose Settings

4. Scroll down to and choose Security

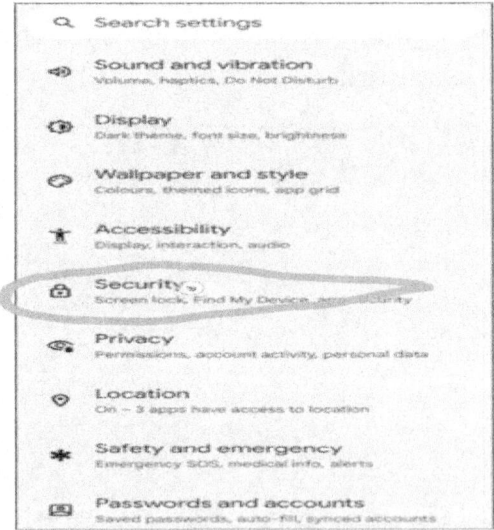

5. Navigate to and choose Advanced settings

6. Choose a SIM card lock

7. Choose Change SIM PIN,

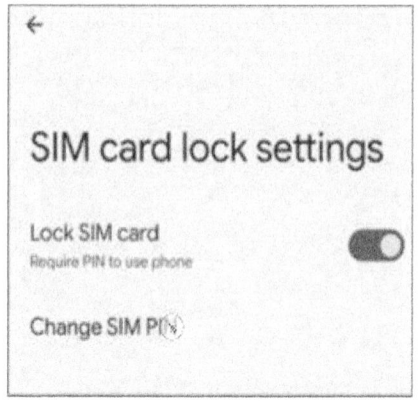

8. Type in your Old SIM PIN, and then click OK

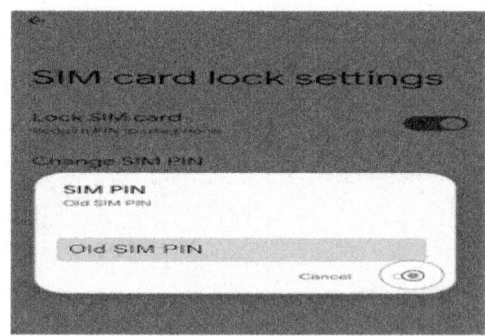

9. Type in your New SIM PIN, then click OK.

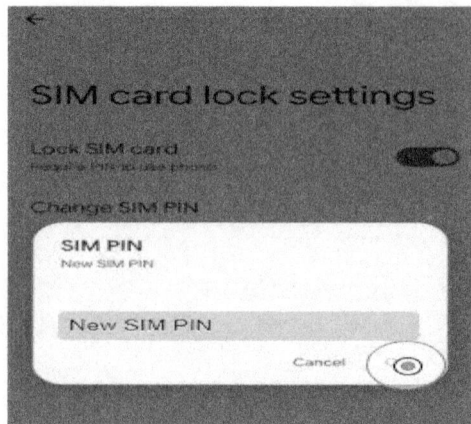

10. Hit on **OK** once you have confirmed your new SIM Passcode.

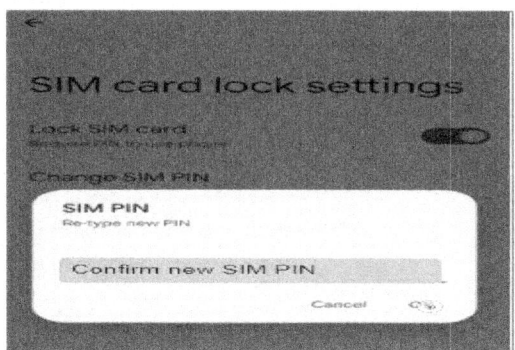

11. A new SIM Password will be allocated to you.

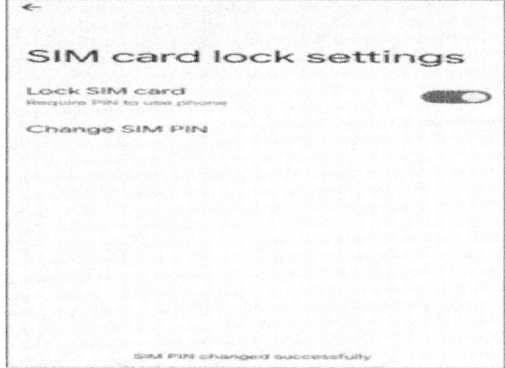

12. Select Screen Lock from the Security menu to turn on your screen lock

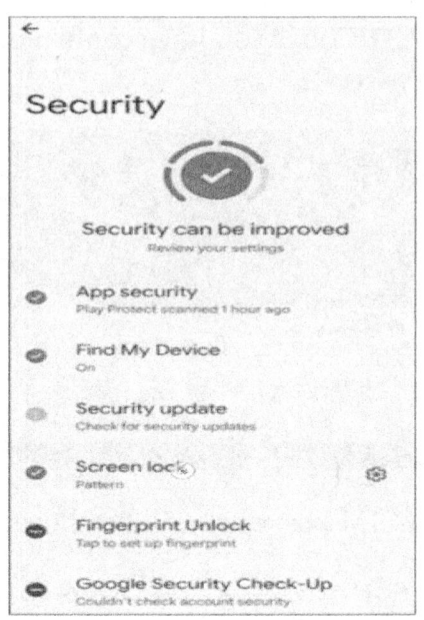

13. Pick a Pattern

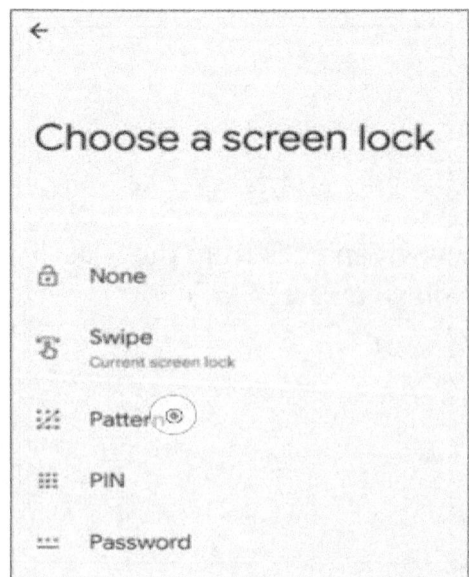

14. Draw an unlock pattern, then choose Next.

15. Draw the unlock pattern once again, then choose Confirm

16. Choose the one you like, then click Done.

17. Now that your phone's screen is locked, it is safe.

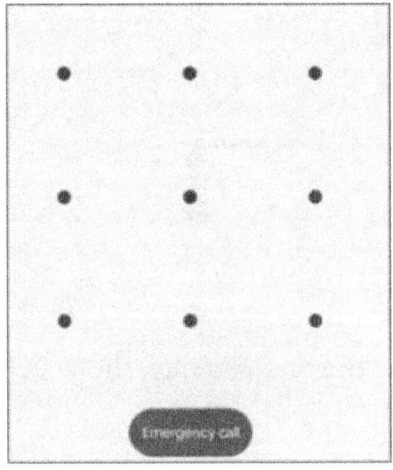

CHAPTER 5

SIM AND e-SIM

Acquire a SIM card and insert it into your Pixel phone

1. Look for a tiny hole in the bottom left corner of your Pixel phone. Fill the hole using the SIM ejection tool that was included with your Pixel phone.

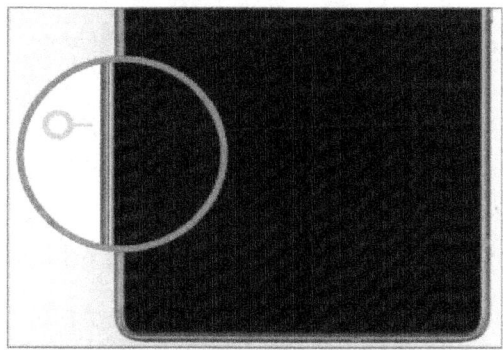

- Just the Pixel 9 series is intended for these instructions. Other devices could have a different location for the SIM tray.
2. Push the tool firmly but gently until the tray comes out.
3. Take away the tray.

- Place the contacts-up side of the nano SIM card in the slot.

4. Put the tray back into its slot gently.

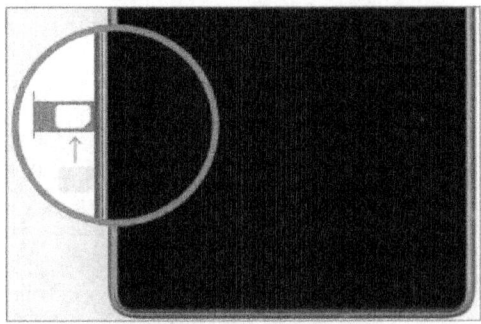

5. Put the tray back into its slot gently

Inserting a SIM card into your gadget

Insert the SIM ejection tool into the little hole on the left edge of the phone.

Note: The SIM card slot is located on the bottom side of your gadget

- Push the tray out with a little touch but firm pressure
- Position the nano SIM card inside the SIM plate after bringing it out
- Put the tray back into its slot gently.
- To acquire mobile service, your phone might need to be restarted. Press the power button for around 3 seconds to restart a mobile phone. Next, choose Restart.

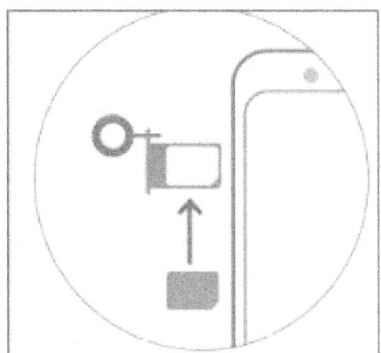

How to utilize a Google Pixel phone with two SIM cards

Add a second SIM card &eSIM

On a device already utilizing a SIM card but not an eSIM:

1. Navigate to and hit on your setup (Settings) application via your gadget
2. Hit Internet & Network
3. Hit on the add or include after the Mobile service network
4. Instead, select Download a SIM
5. Reply to the inquiry "Use or utilize 2 SIM cards?" choose Yes. Your mobile device will update
6. Re-open the Settings application onceyour gadget has been updated
7. Select a Mobile network from the Network & Internet menu
8. Tap your networks to establish call and text choices.

Include a second SIM card

On a phone that has already switched to utilizing an eSIM but no SIM card:

1. Put the SIM card in.
2. Reply to the inquiry, "Use or utilize 2 SIMs?" choose Yes. Your mobile device will update
3. Re-open the Settings application once when your gadget has been updated
4. Select a Mobile network from the Network & Internet menu
5. Tap your networks to establish call and text choices.

Switch SIMs when making calls

You cannot receive a call through the other SIM while you are on a call. Voicemail will be used for calls to the other SIM.

- Data: For that use type, most data is sent through the default SIM. With one exception: When you make a phone call, your SIM handles all data.

Using a SIM that isn't often utilized for data during calls:

- Launch the Settings app
- Click on Network & Internet, then choose SIMs.
- Activate data while on calls.

Turn a SIM off momentarily

To briefly disable a SIM:

1. Navigate to and hit on your setup (Settings) application via your gadget
2. Select a Mobile network from the Network & Internet menu.
3. Choose the SIM you wish to deactivate.
4. Click Use SIM.
5. What comes to mind when you first purchase your new Pixel 9 pro or 8 pro is to switch on your device, After this, you will have to follow the prompt to be able to set up your gadget, as explained below

CHAPTER 6

Motion & Gestures

How to access new gestures and motions, as well as how to use them

Access and modify Quick Settings and notifications

- ACCESS: To get Quick Settings, swipe downward from the Notifications bar. Quick Settings will be presented underneath Notifications

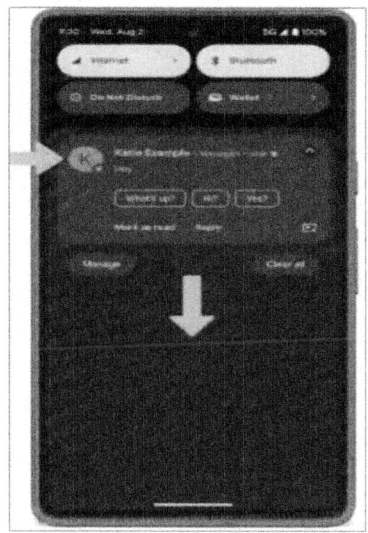

- EDIT APPEARANCE: To access Expanded Quick Settings, swipe down with two fingers from the Notification bar, then tap the edit symbol. Use the desired icon, move it to the desired spot, and then, when you're done, use the Back arrow.

Use extra applications

- To reach the Apps tray, swipe up from the home screen's center.

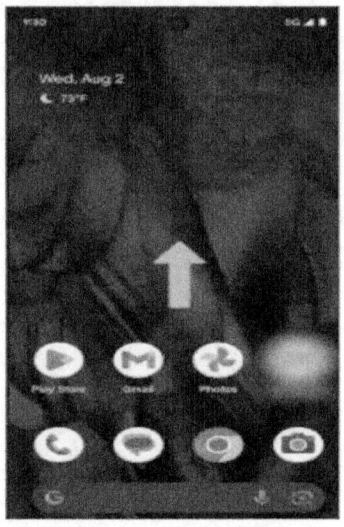

Activate/deactivate gestures

1. Use two fingers to swipe down from the Notification bar, then click the Settings button.
2. After selecting System, choose Gestures

3. To activate or disable the desired gesture, select the desired choice.

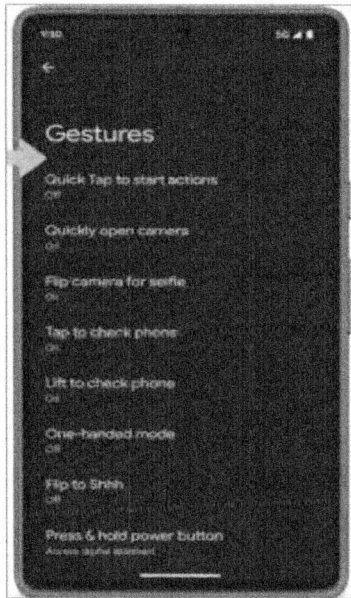

Access and modify navigation bar settings

- **Access:** Swipe down from the notification bar with two fingers, then choose the Settings icon > Display > Navigation mode to alter how you interact with the Navigation bar

- **Edit:** Choose the desired choice from the System navigation panel

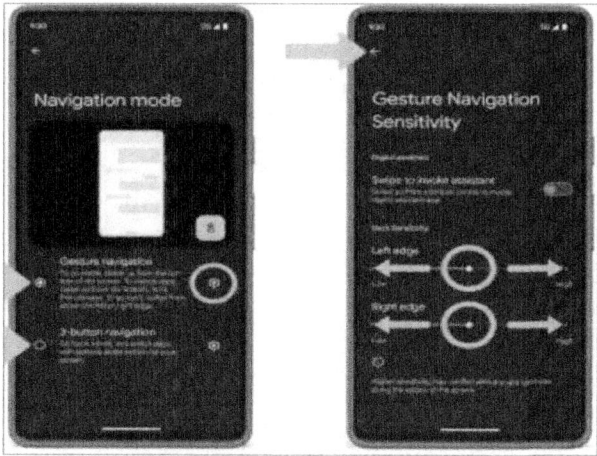

- **Gestures**: To activate a navigation bar that uses gestures, choose Gesture navigation
- **Navigation Buttons:** To enable a navigation bar with buttons, choose 3-button navigation.
- **To Change Gesture Sensitivity**: Click on the Settings button next to Gesture navigation, then choose and drag the Back Sensitivity sliders to the preferred sensitivity. When done, select the back arrow.

Use motions gestures for the full-screen

- Enabling With full-screen motions, you may swipe to go backward and forward, go back to the home screen, check your open applications, and more.
- To navigate home, From the bottom of the screen, swipe upward.

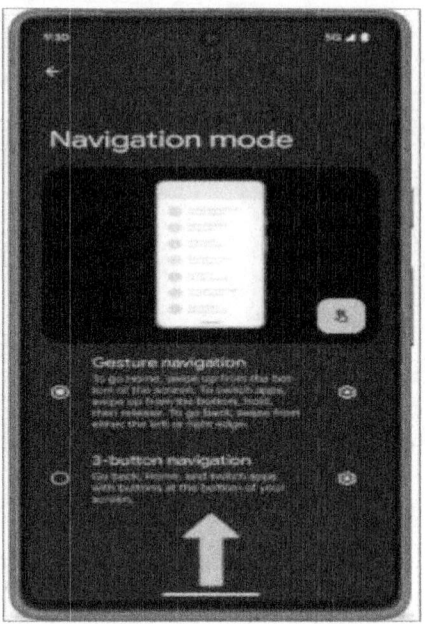

- **Go Back:** From the left or right edge of the screen, swipe in toward the center of the screen.

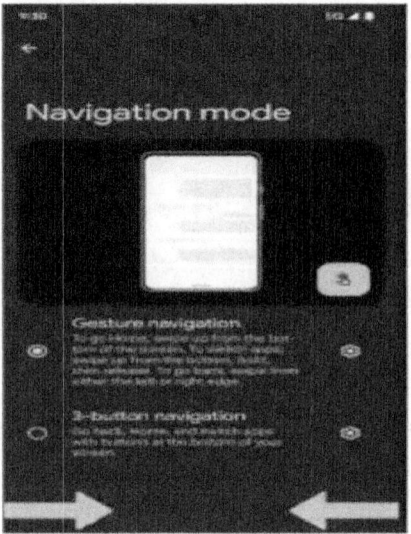

- **Advanced Apps**: Keep holding your finger on the screen while you swipe up from the bottom border.

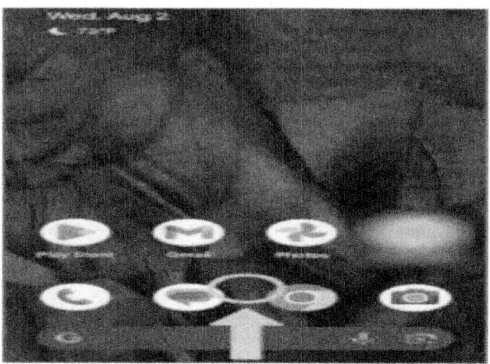

- Alternate between apps: swipe either left or right.

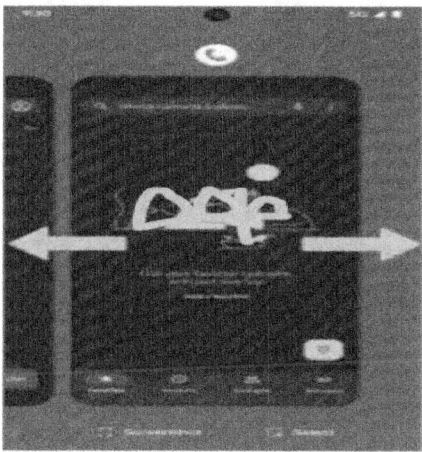

Utilize Quick Tap

You may take action by double-tapping the back of your phone if Quick Tap is enabled. Choose Quick Tap to initiate activities from the Gestures panel to enable this gesture. Choose the required action after selecting the Use Quick Tap switch.

Utilise flip to mute

You may quiet the phone when it is face down by enabling Flip to mute.

1. Navigate to setting
2. Hit on the motion and gesture panel
3. Hit on the flip to mute logo to make this gesture active

CHAPTER 7

Internet and Cellular Info

See the signal strength of the cellular network and control mobile data, international roaming, and cellular data use.

Check your network connection's strength

1. **CONNECTION TYPE:** The Notification bar's Network symbol will appear when you're connected to 5G.
2. **CONNECTION STRENGTH**: The strength of the connection is shown by the signal bars. The stronger the connection, the more bars that are visible.

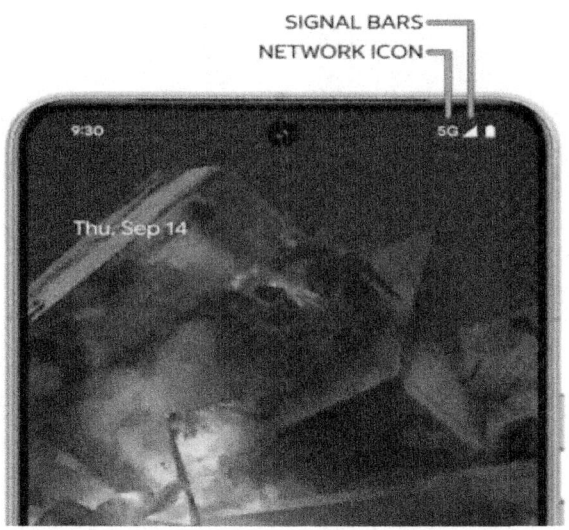

Accessing your cellular data

1. Using two fingers, swipe down from the Notification bar and choose the Settings icon
2. Choose Internet > Network & Internet. Choose the Settings icon located adjacent to your network

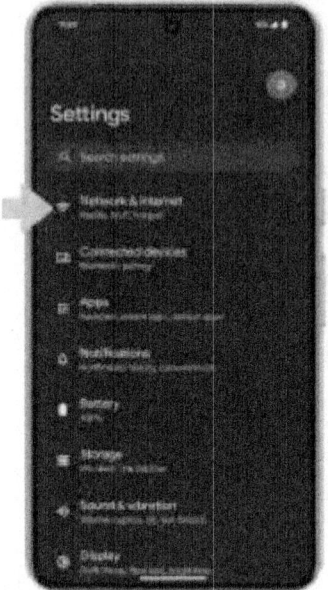 

Activate or deactivate mobile data

1. Choose the switch for mobile data.

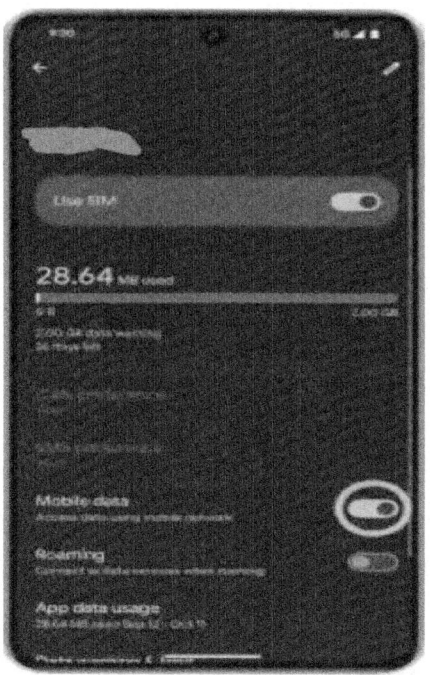

Turn on or off international data

1. Choose the Roaming switch from the Mobile Data panel.

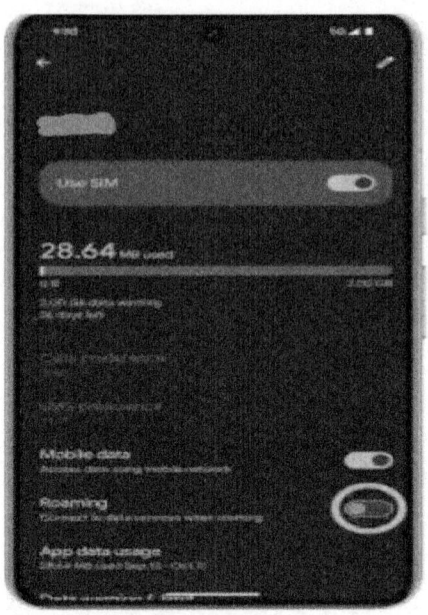

Toggle on or off mobile data quickly

1. Swipe two fingers down from the Notification bar.
2. Click the symbol for the Internet
3. And choose your network switch.

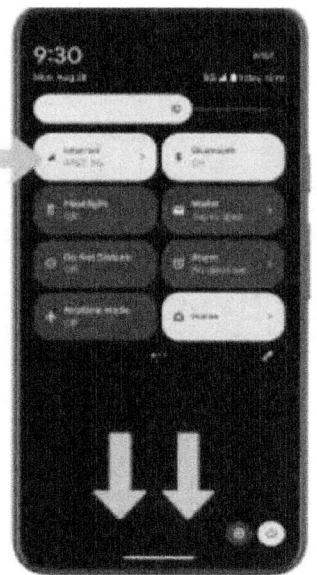 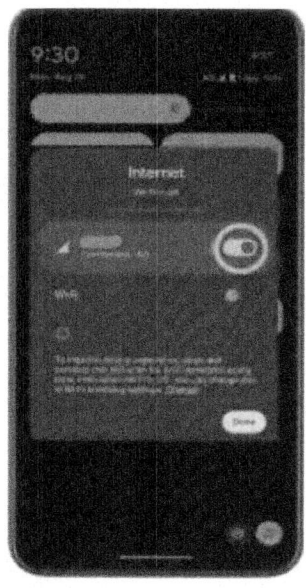

Browsing the Internet (web)

You can surf the internet, access or modify bookmarks, open tabs, and modify browser settings.

Accessing the major Browser
1. Navigate to the Chrome app picture icon and
2. Click on it.

Go to website
1. Type the address of the desired website into the search bar and
2. Press the Enter keys

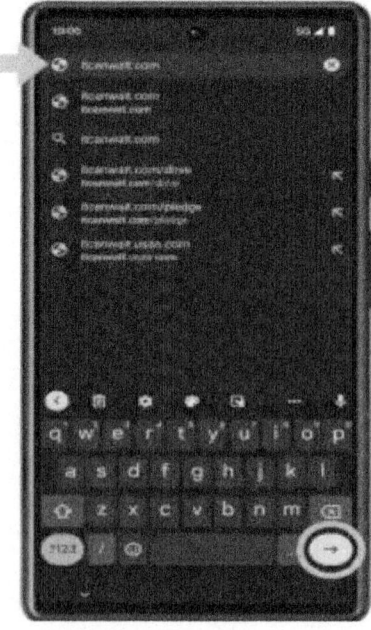

Bookmark website

Depending on your device,

1. Choose the Menu dots or Menu lines image icon before choosing the Bookmark symbol to bookmark a website.
2. Click on Bookmarks to view bookmarks

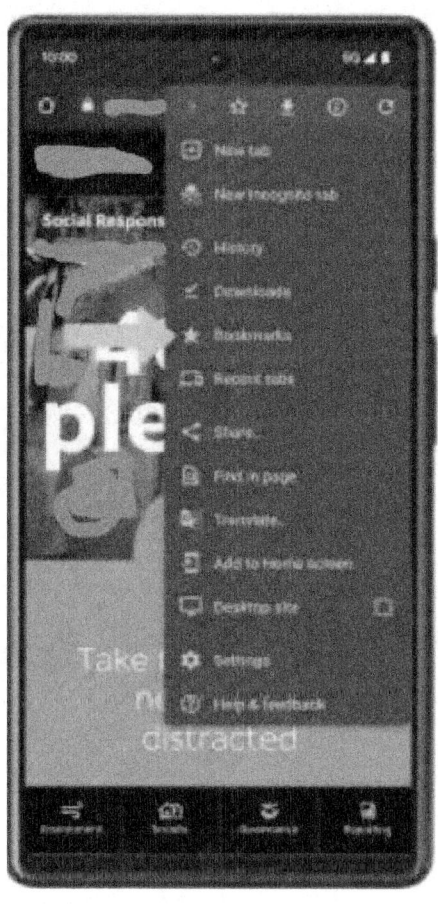

Access/open/close browser tabs

1. Via the browser display, choose the tabs symbol to navigate the presently launched or opened tabs
2. Choose the add symbol to launch a fresh tab
3. Click the X symbol to end a tab.

Accessing your browser setup

You may change font size, modify the default home page, block and allow pop-ups, and erase history by going into your browser's settings.

1. Choose the Menu dots or Menu lines picture icon from the browser.
2. Using the menu icon on your smartphone, scroll to and choose Settings.

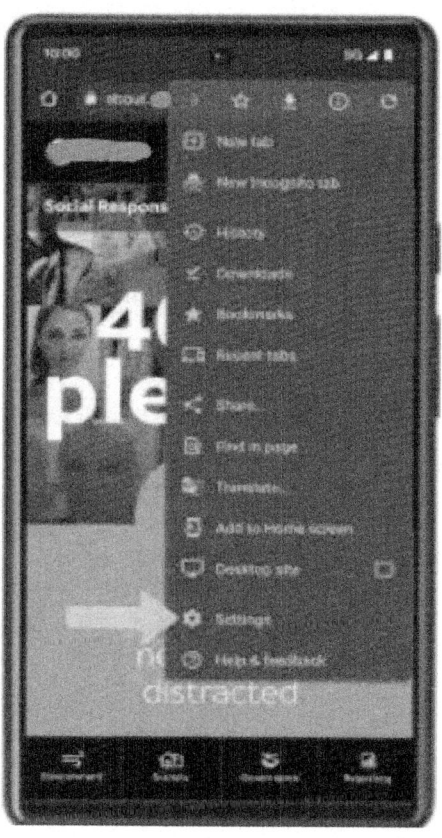

WiFi/hotspot settings &usage

Wi-Fi may be turned on, off, connected to, and disconnected from networks.

Make use of WiFi

To access the Internet,

1. From the Notification bar, swipe downwards,
2. choose the wifi& hold the wifi symbol

Join a wireless network (wifi)

To activate Wi-Fi services if it's deactivated,

1. Turn on the Wi-Fi switch. Once Wi-Fi is turned on, choose the network you want to connect to.

Note: After entering the Wi-Fi password and choosing Connect, if you're connected to a secure network. A lock icon will be displayed for secure networks.

Forget a Network service

1. Next to the preferred network, tap the Settings button, then
2. Choose Forget

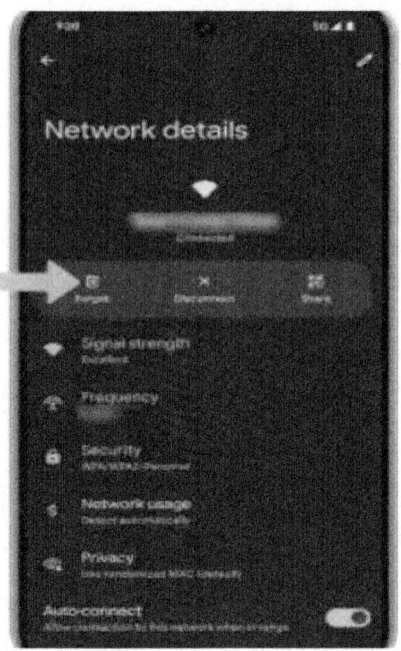

Connecting to a secret network

1. Select Add network from the Wi-Fi screen by clicking on the network list at the bottom

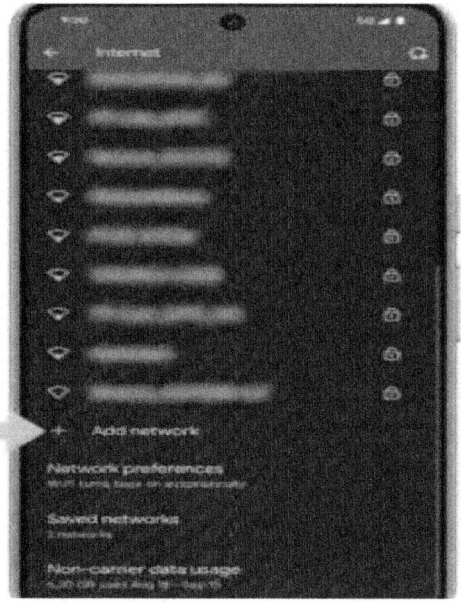

Note: To proceed after connecting to a secret network, you will be asked to provide the network's SSID, security type, and password (if applicable)

Mobile (portable) Hotspot

1. Configure your gadget as a personal hotspot and allow other Wi-Fi-enabled devices to use your internet connection.
   - The Mobile Hotspot symbol will appear in the Notification bar when activated.

Activate/deactivate mobile hotspot

1. Using two fingers, swipe down from the Notification bar and choose the Settings icon
2. Choose Hotspot & tethering after selecting Network & internet

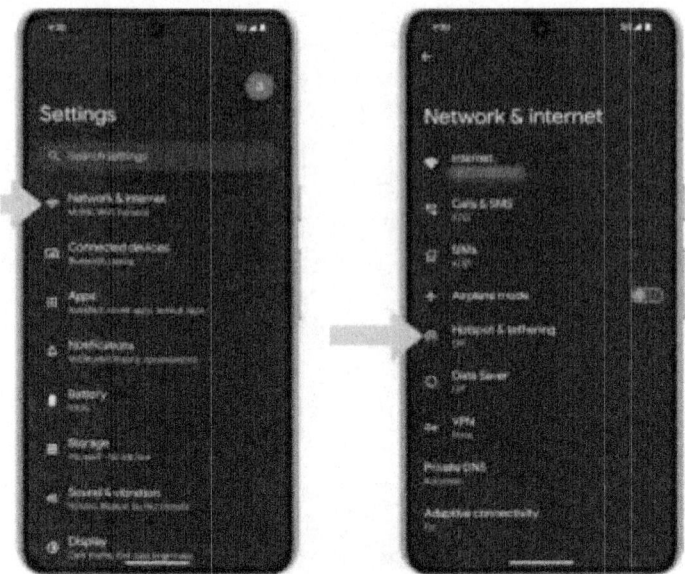

3. To turn the Wi-Fi hotspot on or off, choose the switch.

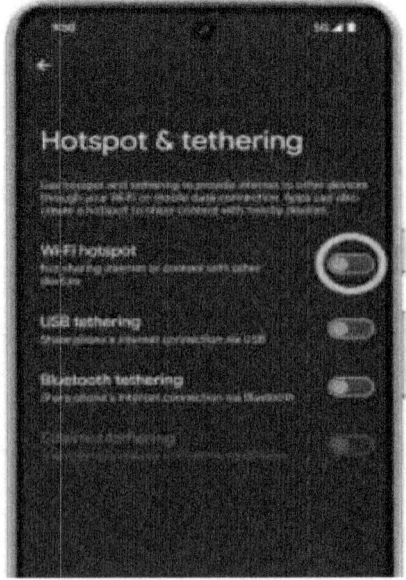

Set up the Mobile Hotspot settings

1. Choose the preferred network configuration from the Wi-Fi hotspot screen:

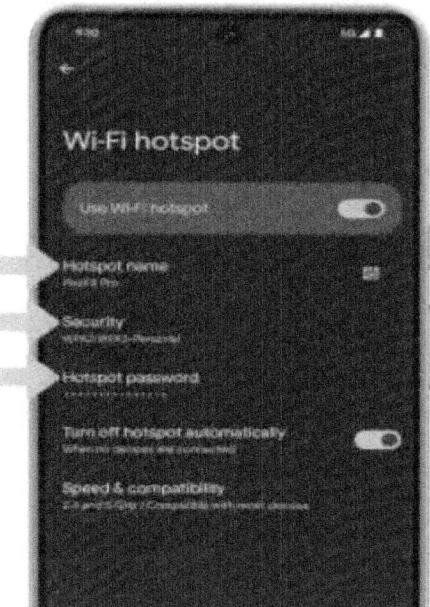

- **Hotspot name:** Modify the Mobile Hotspot network's name
- **Security**: Modify the mobile hotspot network's security type
- **Hotspot password**: Modify the mobile hotspot network's password

2. Once the appropriate information has been edited, choose OK.

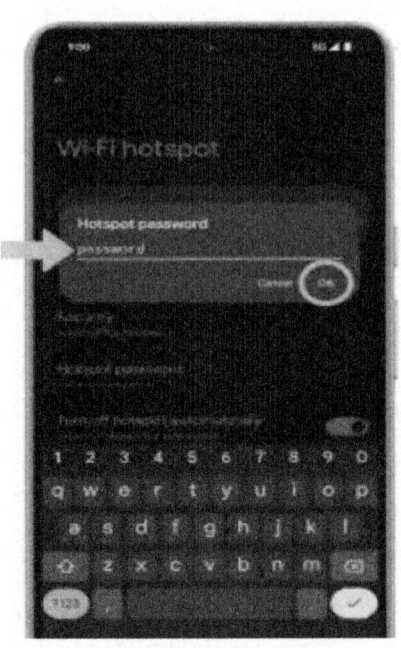

CHAPTER 8

Connectivity

Bluetooth

Switch Bluetooth On & off Using the Settings app

1. Go to the setup on your gadget (setup application)
2. Select Bluetooth from the list of connected devices, followed by Connection Preferences
3. Switch on or off Bluetooth

Switch Bluetooth on or off via quick settings

1. Via the upper section of the display, slide downward
2. The Bluetooth Quick Settings tile can be touched, tapped, or held in place:
   - Tap: Unlocks the three Bluetooth devices that you most recently linked.
   - Invert Turn on or off Bluetooth.
   - Touch and hold: Brings up the Settings app's "Connected devices" tab.
   - Select Bluetooth from the Connection Preferences menu.
   - Turn on or off Use Bluetooth.

Utilizehotspot tethering in sharing connection

You may access the Internet on a different phone, tablet, or computer by using the mobile data on your phone.

Use Bluetooth to tether

1. Link your phone and the other gadgets together
2. Configure the second device to use Bluetooth to establish a network connection.
3. Go to the setup on your gadget (setup application)
4. Select Internet and Network. Next, tethering and hotspot
5. Select "Tethering" via Bluetooth.

Tethering via USB cable

Important: Android devices cannot be tethered via USB to Mac PCs.

1. Attach your phone to the other device using a USB cord. At the top of the screen, there is a notification that reads "Connected as a."
2. Navigate to the setup (Settings) application on your phone
3. Select Network and Internet, followed by Tethering and Hotspot.
4. Switch on tethering via USB

Transfer files via your device

Wireless data transfer

1. Establish a connection with both phones.
2. Activate both of your Android phones.
3. On your new Android phone, adhere to the on-screen directions.
4. Choose your information.
5. To add your Google Account and activate your SIM, follow the on-screen prompts.
6. Select the files you want to copy from your current Android phone.
7. transfer.Data
8. And that's it! Your new Android phone now has your data on it.

CHAPTER 9

Live Translate

Discover how to utilize Google Assistant, Live Caption, and Live Translate on text messages, and the camera.

Turn on Live Translation

1. Utilizing 2 fingers, slide downward via the Notification bar & touch the Settings logo
2. Navigate to System > Choose Live Translate > Press the Live Translate switch.

Note: Real-time audio and conversation translation is provided by Google Tensor. Translations will show up next to the audio when you're messaging, on the phone, or viewing videos.

3. After choosing Add a Language, click the Download button next to the language you want to use

Note: To confirm, click Add language when requested. Toggling the relevant switch under the Translate from the section on the Live Translate screen will activate or disable the language after the add-on has been downloaded.

4. Choose Translate to and then pick the preferred choice.

Note: To confirm, select language

Using Live Translation on Text Messages

1. Select the Messages app from the home screen
2. Locate and pick the preferred message thread by scrolling
3. Choose the desired message, hold it, and then click the Copy icon

Note: Selecting the Copy symbol will cause another icon to show up, which will translate the desired content. To translate your message on screen in the language of your choice, select Translate to English or Translate copied text at the top of the screen.

4. Choose the Menu icon first, then the Translate icon, once the on-screen keyboard appears
5. Insert the copied text into the section labeled "Type here to translate." The text message area will show the translated message.

Translate using the camera

1. Select Lens from the Home screen. To access Translate, swipe left
2. When a photo is taken, the camera will automatically identify any foreign languages and provide the translation on the screen

Translate a discussion into a foreign language using Google Assistant

1. Hold down the Power/Lock knob & click it all over to pop up Google Assistant. Ask that Google Translate "translate discussion"
2. Click the Choose Language drop-down menu, then pick the preferred choice

Note: You may also specify the language you want to translate from and out of with Google Assistant.

3. Touch the microphone logo. Press the microphone icon to begin speaking. It will show the translation.

Use Live Captioning when watching media in any language

1. Utilizing 2 fingers, slide downward via the Notification bar & touch the Settings logo
2. Go to Accessibility, choose Live Caption, then click the Use Live Caption option
3. Locate and modify the settings as needed.

CHAPTER 10

Multitask with your device

Using split-screen modes on Pixel 9

What does split-screen mode mean?

You may display two programs side by side on the phone screen with Android's built-in split-screen mode. Like a desktop computer, it lets you do a lot of things, like read an article or social network feed while watching a YouTube video, compose a message on WhatsApp while seeing a recipe in another window, and much more.

Open two applications at once

Depending on the model and operating system of your phone, the split-screen mode may go by different names, but the instructions for enabling it are often the same as the ones on the Pixel phone below:

1. Use the menu bar button or screen gestures to access the Recent Applications panel
2. Press the application's icon

3. Select the option for Split Screen
4. Choose which other program to use to divide the screen.

  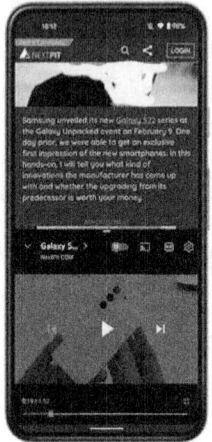

Using an app to launch in a pop-up window

Additional multitasking options are also available on some phones and system skins. For example, you may open an application as a floating window or pop-up view.

1. Navigate to the Recent Apps window.
2. Press the application's icon
3. Choose to Open in a pop-up window.

Accessing your device's split screen

1. Swipe up from the bottom of the screen while keeping your finger on it to see the most recent apps.

Click the split screen after selecting the preferred program icon.

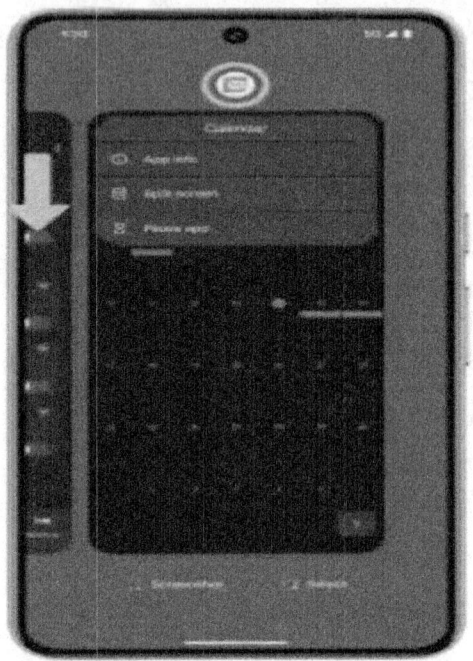

Note: Split screens will only be available in compatible apps.

2. Choose whatever app you want to see in the window at the bottom

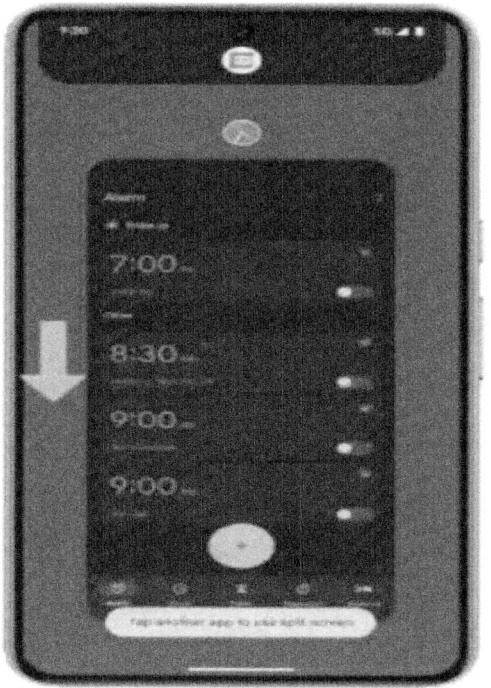

Note: The Calendar and Contacts apps were chosen for this example.

Modify the window's size

- Choose the Divider symbol in the center of the screen.
- Move it up or down to your preferred position, and then let go.

Note that, depending on which program you wish to launch in its entirety, you may drag the divider symbol from the top or bottom of the screen.

Leave the Split Screen

While your finger remains on the screen,

1. Slide up from the screen's bottom.
2. To remove the split-screen window, select it and drag it up.

 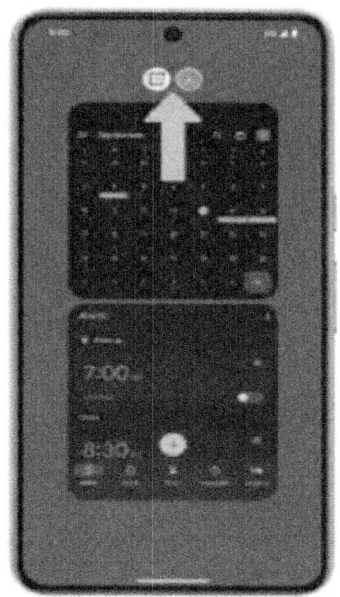

Using Picture-in-Picture

1. Swipe up from the bottom of the screen while using full-screen applications like Google Maps, Duo, YouTube, or Chrome. The application will appear in the corner of the screen as a Picture-in-Picture window.

 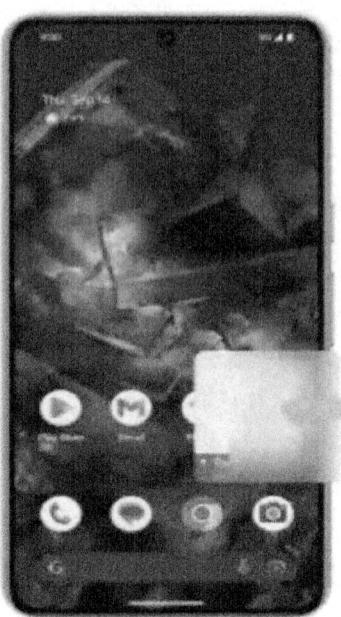

Note: You are free to choose how to drag the window. Some apps come with picture-in-picture enabled by default. From the notification bar, swipe downward using two fingers. choose the Settings icon, then choose Applications > Special app access > Picture-in-picture. A list of apps that support Picture-in-picture will appear.

CHAPTER 11

Photos and Videos

Accessing and Archiving Your Photos and Videos

1. Hit on the Gallery icon via the camera application.

Camera and Video Presets

Accessing camera settings on your gadget

- Choose the camera application via the home screen, then
- Slide downward via the upper section of the screen.

- To view other camera options, select More Settings.

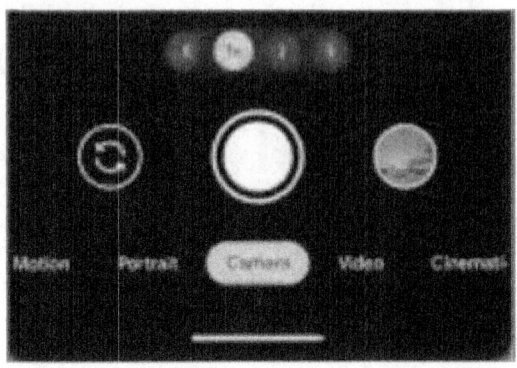

Adjust or modify your photo's size

1. Choose the preferred ratio from the camera's settings menu.

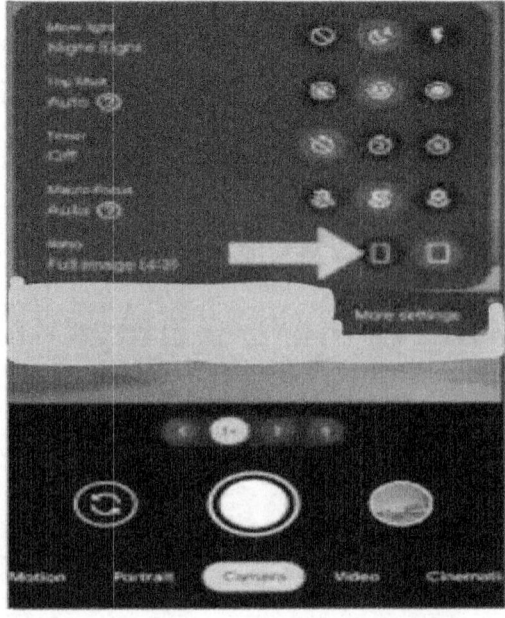

On/Off the flash switch

1. Choose the preferred flash setting from the camera's settings menu.

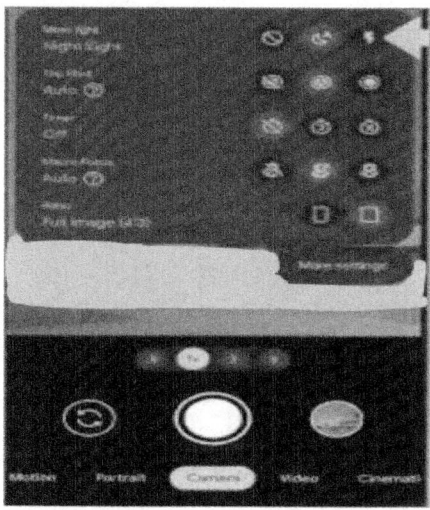

Place a timer

1. Choose the preferred time from the camera's settings menu.

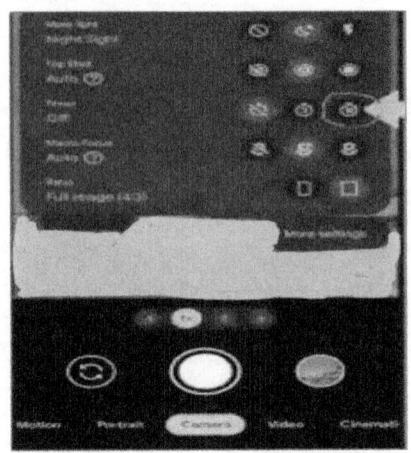

Access the camera and microphone for editing

1. Slide two fingers downward via the Notification bar & then leftward.
2. Toggle it on or off by choosing the Mic access or Camera access icons, respectively.

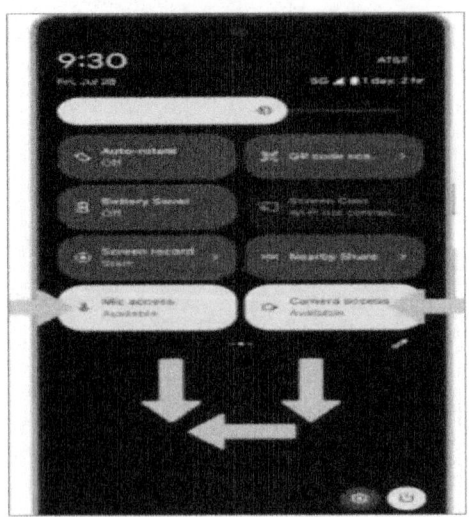

Snapping a screenshot

Learn how to access and take screen captures.

Snap a screenshot

1. Hold down the Volume Down and Power/Lock buttons at the same time.

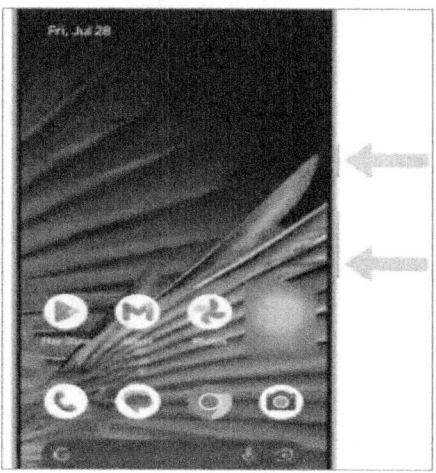

Editing or sharing screenshots instantly

A notification will show up on the screen just after you take a snapshot. Choose the preferred choice:

- **Edit a Screenshot**: Click the Edit icon, then make the necessary changes to the screenshot.
- **Share a Screenshot**: Click the Share icon, then adhere to the sharing instructions.

Access and use screen recording

You can record what is happening on your phone's screen.

Start recording

1. Slide downward via the notification panel
2. Slide leftward
3. Hit on the Screen to record the logo
4. Change, modify, or adjust settings as needed, then
5. Click Start.

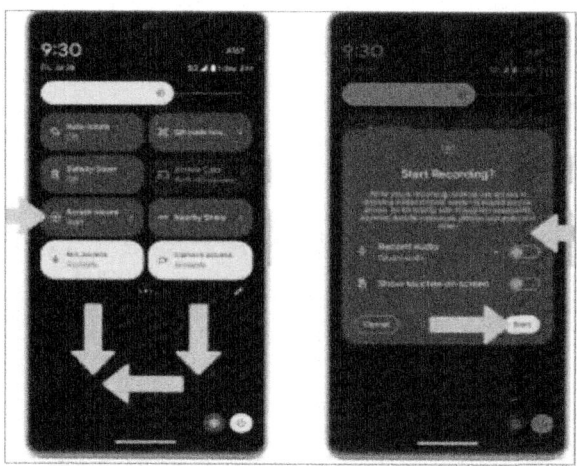

End recording

1. Slide downward via the Notifications panel
2. Hit on the Stop logo on the Screen Recorder notification, and the recording will end.

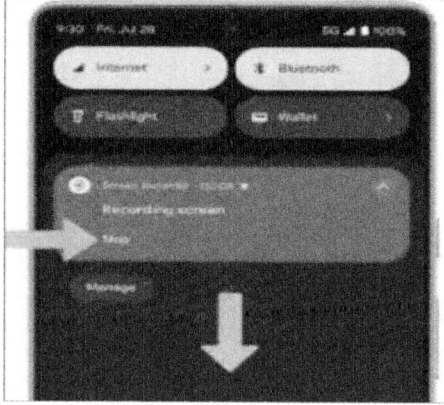

Transfer your videos and photos

Transfer files between a PC and your device.

Media transfer to or via a PC

1. Put the USB-C end of the USB-C cable into the port on the bottom of the device when it is turned on. Insert the USB end of the USB-C cable into an accessible computer port.

2. Swipe down from the notification bar,
3. Choose Android System from the drop-down menu, Charging notification, then File transfer, Android Auto, or PTP to put the smartphone in the proper USB mode
4. Select This PC after clicking the File Explorer icon
5. After selecting the device name, go to the specified folder

6. To transfer files, drag and drop them onto or from the device disc.

Transferring files to or via Macs

1. To facilitate the connection between your device and a Mac computer, you need the Android File Transfer program. Install the Android File Transfer app after downloading it.

2. With the device switched on, connect the USB-C cable's other end to the port. Insert the USB end of the USB-C cable into an accessible computer port.

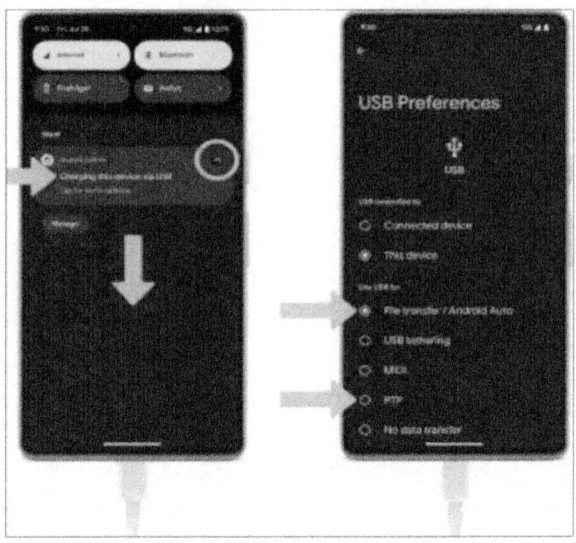

3. Swipe down from the notification bar, choose Android System from the drop-down menu, Charging notification, then choose File transfer, Android Auto, or PTP to put the smartphone in the proper USB mode
4. The Android File Transfer software will launch instantly once the phone is connected to the computer. Choose the folder you want to move files to/from
5. Drag and drop the files you want to transfer to or from the device.

Advanced Photos & Videos

Access the camera's modes

1. Navigate and slide to the camera application
2. Now slide leftward or rightward in the Camera app to access features including Night Sight, Portrait, Video, cinematic, panorama, photo share, lens, etc.

Customize photo and video settings

1. Navigate to the Camera application
2. Slide downward to access the settings
3. Modify, edit, or adjust settings as preferred
4. Hit on More settings for other available camera setups

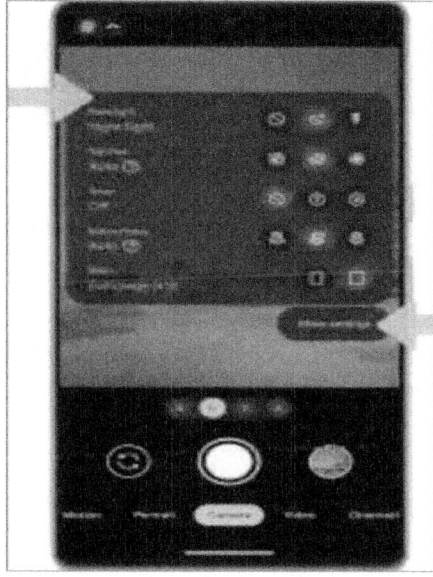

Activate or deactivate the shutter sound

1. Navigate to the camera application
2. Then navigate to the camera settings display screen
3. Hit on the camera sound switch

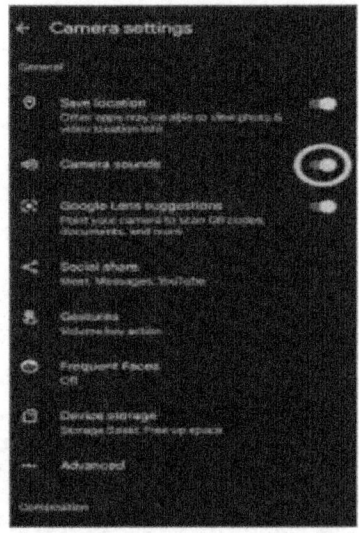

Crop a picture

1. Click the Gallery icon from the Camera app.
2. Select the Edit icon after sliding to the appropriate picture.
3. Pick a crop. Choose and move the crop corners to achieve the desired crop, then choose Save.

Utilize filters

1. Swipe left on the lower section of the editing screen to access Filters.
2. To apply, choose Save Copy after selecting the desired filter.

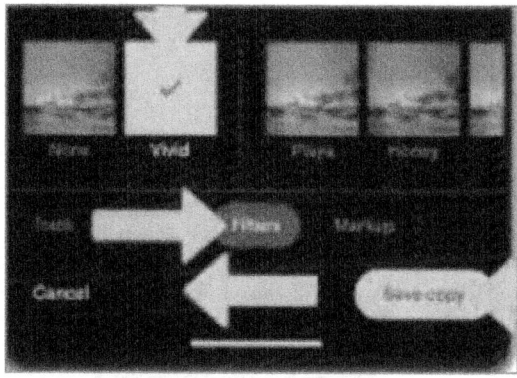

Using a magic eraser

1. To choose the magic eraser when editing a photo, swipe left on the bottom area to Tools.

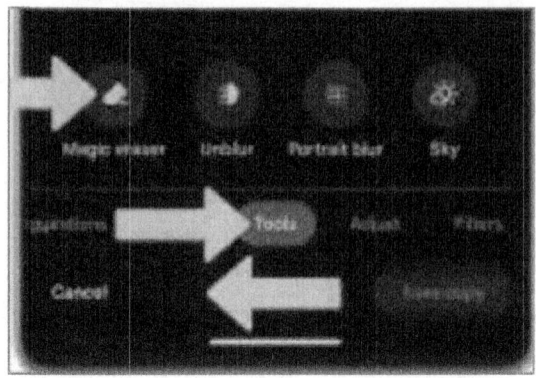

2. To delete a portion of the image, circle or select it
3. Choose the preferred choice while using the magic eraser tool to edit:
    - RESET: To restore the picture to its initial condition, choose Reset.
    - UNDO: Press the Undo menu.
    - REDO: Click the button for Redo

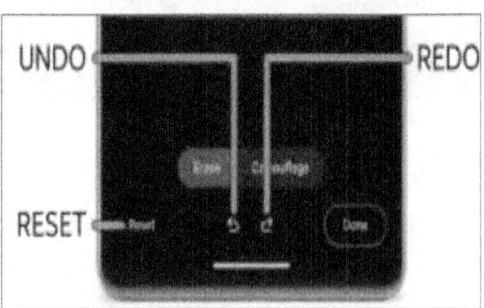

4. Click Done when done.

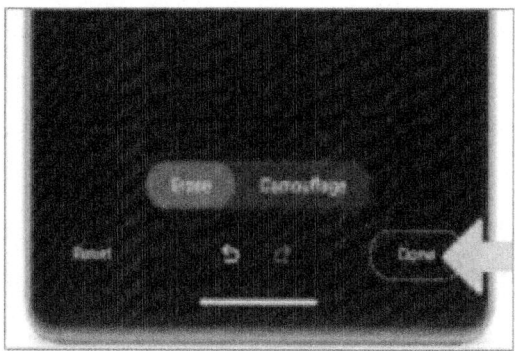

Utilize Photo Un-blur

1. Swipe left via the lower section of the editing screen to access Tools, then

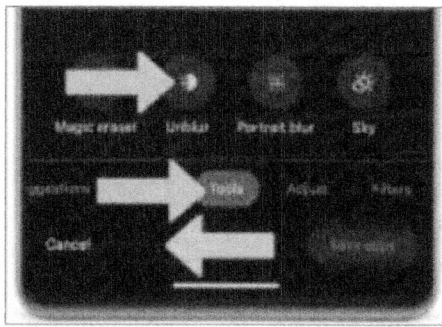

2. Choose Unblur
3. Tap Done after swiping left or right to change the effect's strength as desired

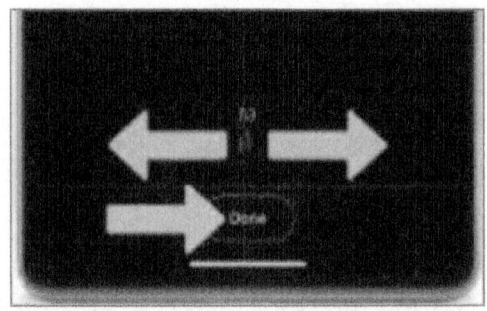

Utilize Night Vision

1. Navigate to the camera application
2. Slide your finger rightward on the screen to Night Sight
3. Hit on the Capture icon, then
4. Hold the camera perfectly still for roughly 5 seconds.

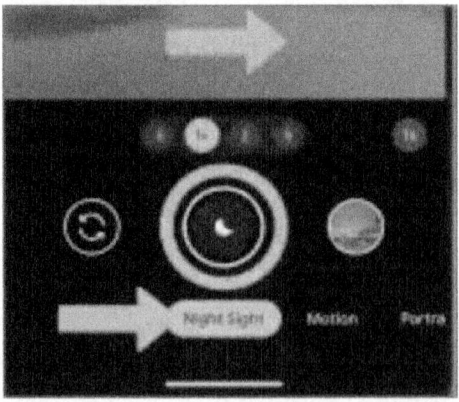

Utilize the Motion mode

1. Navigate to the camera application
2. Slide rightward to motion
3. Hit on the preferred motion capture option mode

4. Hit on the motion record logo

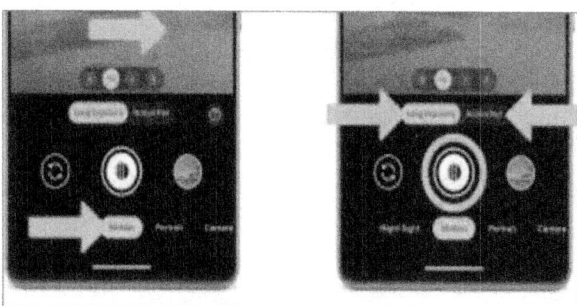

Use photo effects

1. Click the Gallery icon from the Camera app. Select the Edit icon after sliding to the appropriate picture.
2. To blur pictures, use the Blur tool. Choose Tools, then choose Blur. To change the focus as required, select the desired spot on the screen, then click Done
3. To get rid of any obtrusive elements in images, use Magic Eraser. Draw a circle around the undesirable aspects by selecting and dragging, then click Done
4. To correct skin tones in photographs, use Skin Tone. Select Skin Tone after choosing Adjust. Choose Done after dragging the Skin Tone slider to the desired position.

Create a video or take pictures

Take a picture

Learn how to use your device to shoot pictures or videos.

1. Navigate to the camera application
2. Hit on the Capture button.

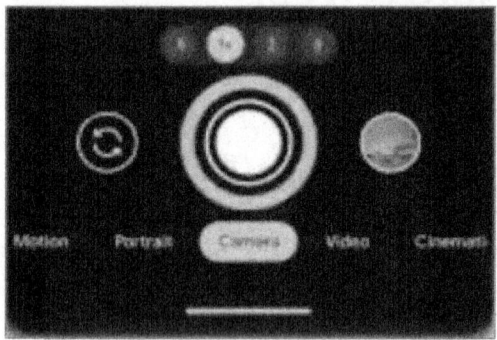

Note: You could also press one of the Volume buttons.

Swapping between the front-facing and rear-facing cameras

1. Navigate to the camera application
2. Select the camera-switch symbol.

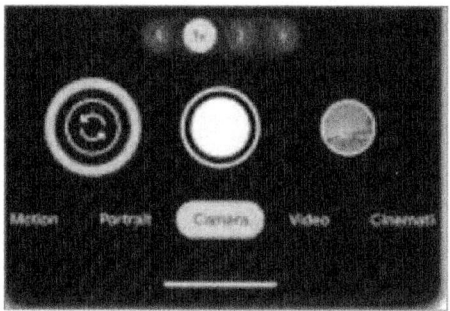

Adjust the camera's focus
1. Navigate to the camera application
2. To focus the camera, choose the desired spot on the screen.

Zoom in and out
- To zoom in, move two fingers around the screen's perimeter, starting at the center

- Then drag out.
- To zoom out, pinch two fingers from the screen's outer edges to its center.

Activate the Macro mode

To change the Macro Focus setting, swipe down from the top of the screen. You can capture finely detailed up-close images and films with macro focus.

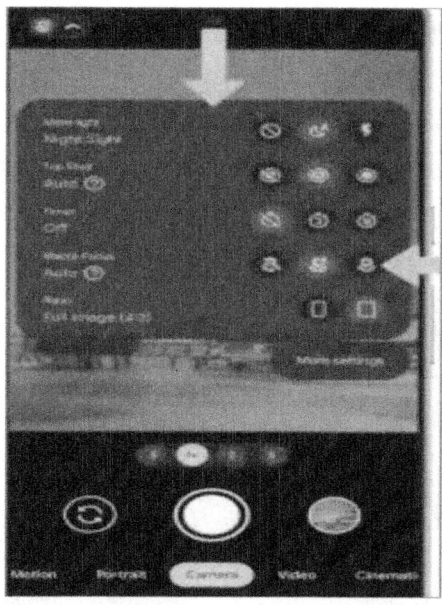

Access Night Sight and utilize it

1. Navigate to the camera application
2. Slide your finger rightward to Night Sight in the Camera app.
3. Hit on the Capture logo, then
4. Hold the camera perfectly still for roughly 5 seconds.

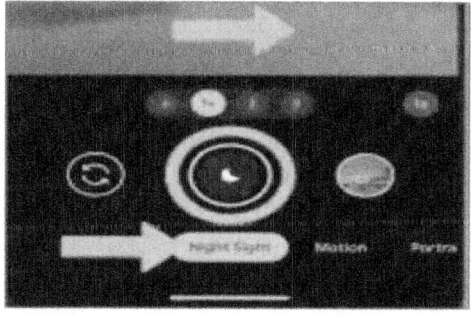

Use and access Picture Sphere

1. Photo Sphere enables you to stitch together several photographs to produce a 360-degree image. Swipe left to Modes in the Camera app, then choose Photo Sphere to start using the Photo Sphere option
2. Click the Camera icon, then follow the instructions to take pictures of your surroundings. Select the Checkmark icon when done.

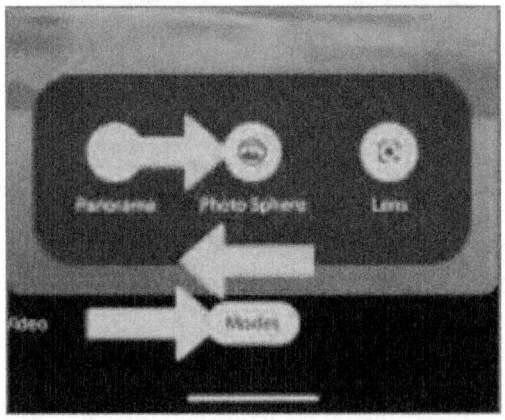

Use and access Panorama

By fusing many shots, a panorama enables you to take broader pictures.

1. Navigate to the camera application
2. Swipe left to Modes in the Camera app,
3. Then choose Panorama to launch panorama mode.
4. To finish the capture, choose the Capture icon and pan the camera.

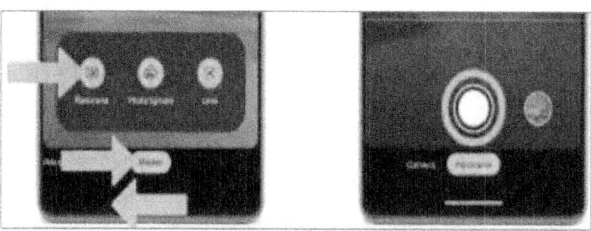

Access and utilize Google Lens

- ACCESS: Tap Lens in the Modes section of the Camera app by swiping left
- USE: Aim your device's camera at a certain object or area, then swipe left or right to activate the Google Lens function of your choice and follow the on-screen instructions. In addition to looking up homework questions, translating, copying text from images, and looking up comparable items or locations, Google Lens can also look up products and locations.

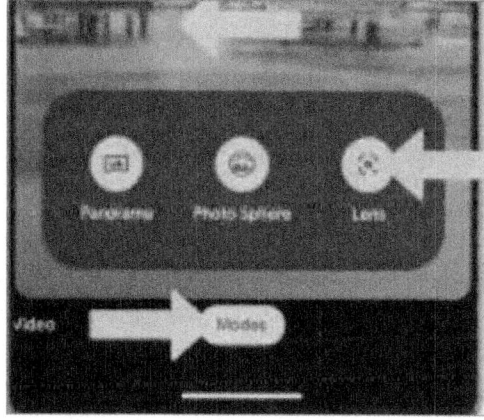

Record a Video

Recording or Making a video

1. To start recording, swipe left to enter video mode.
    - You can select between various video styles, including time-lapse and Slow Motion.
2. To record videos in slow motion, click the Slow Motion button and then choose the desired recording speed
3. To record videos quickly, click the Time Lapse icon and then choose the number of frames you want to capture.

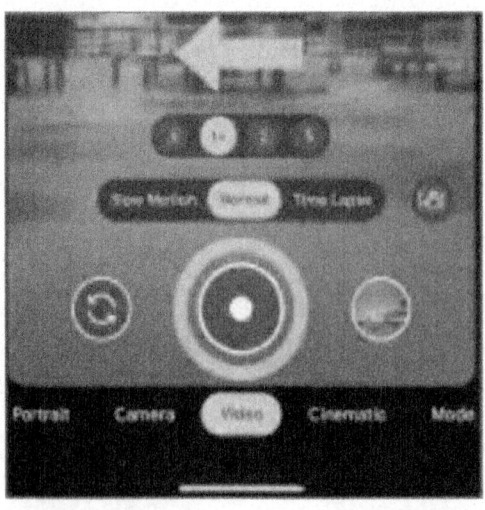

Stop, pause, and resume a recording

To pause the video,
1. Select the Pause button. To stop the recording, use the Stop button.
2. To Resume a recording, hit on the Record logo.

Snap a still picture while in video mode
1. Navigate to the camera application
2. Switch to video recording
3. Hit the red Capture button.

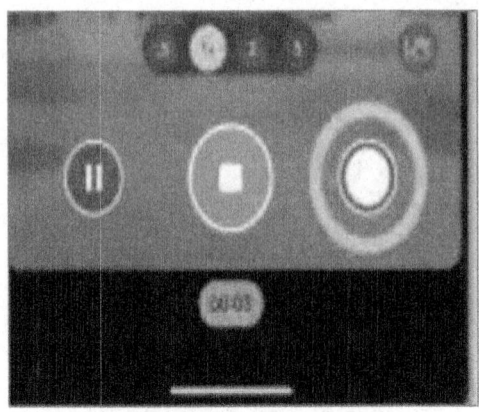

Utilize Slow Motion

Video may be captured in Slow Motion at a slower playing speed.

1. Navigate to your gadget camera application
2. Switch to video mode
3. Select Slow Motion, then choose the preferred playback speed choice, all while the Camera app is in video mode.

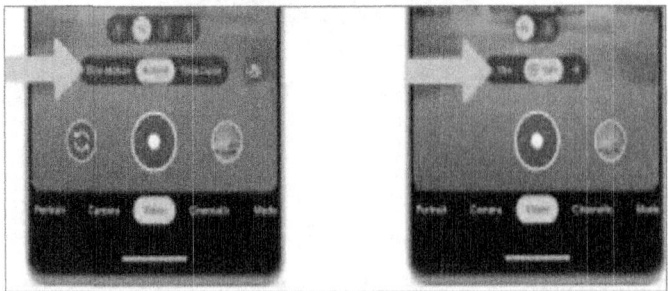

Utilize Time Lapse

Videos may be recorded using time-lapse at a quicker playing speed.

1. Go to your device's camera application.
2. Switch to video
3. Hit on Time Lapse and then the preferred playback speed when the Camera app is in video mode.

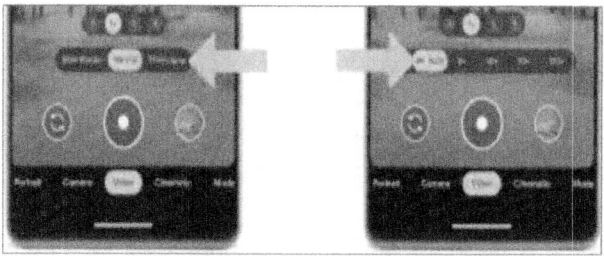

Super-res Zoom

Toggle Super-res zoom without turning it on or going to a specific place. Simply zoom past the default focal length, and it should be activated.

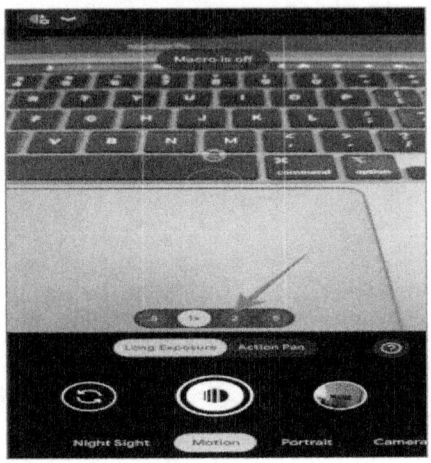

Cinematic Mode

1. Launch the Pixel 9 pro or Pixel 9 pro's Camera app.in the first step.

2. On the bottom bar, swipe twice to the left. You will enter Cinematic Mode after doing so.

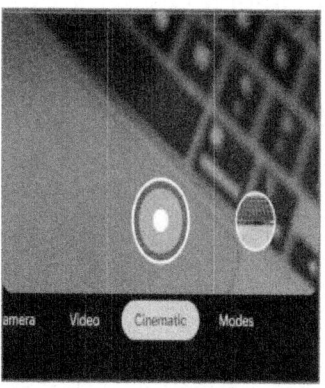

3. At this point, tap the topic you want to concentrate on. Start recording after that.

Cinematic Pan

1. Launch the Pixel 9 pro or Pixel 9 pro's Camera app. in the first step

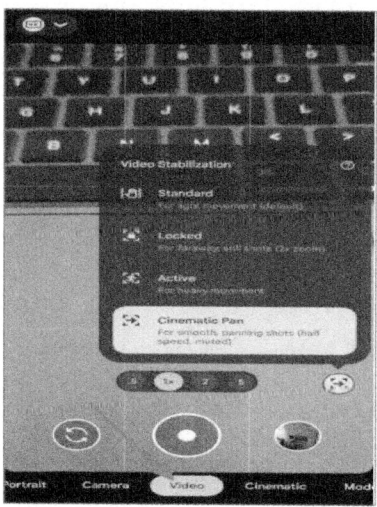

2. Once on the bottom bar, swipe to the left. You are now in video mode
3. Tap the symbol for stabilization. Select Cinematic Pan next.

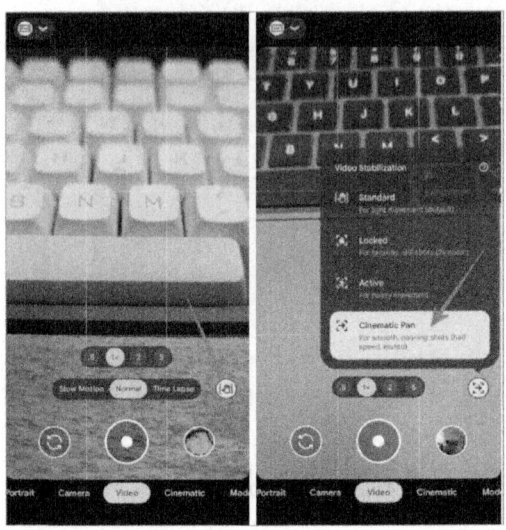

While filming professionally or while attempting to produce a video for a product display, you can use this mode.

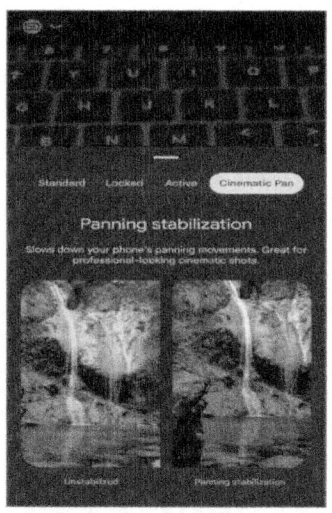

Active Stabilization

1. Launch the Pixel 9 pro or Pixel 9 pro's Camera app. in the first step.
2. Once on the bottom bar, swipe to the left. You are now in video mode

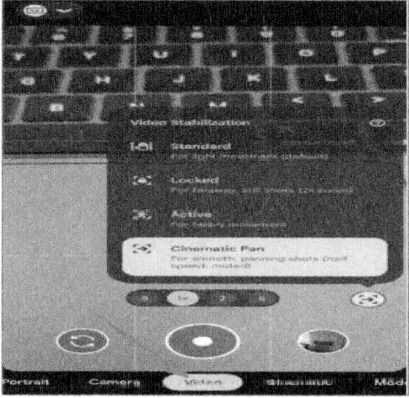

3. Tap the symbol for stabilization. Choose Active next.

You now know which stabilization mode to choose the next time you want to record your POV while biking or surfing.

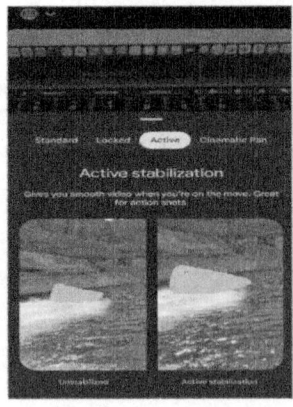

Action Pan

1. Launch the Pixel 9 pro or Pixel 9 pro's Camera app. in the first step
2. On the bottom bar, swipe twice to the right. You are now in motion mode

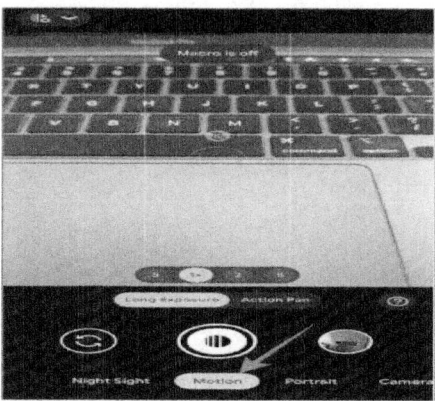

3. To change to the appropriate mode, use the Action Pan button

4. From this point forward, anytime you detect a moving subject, press the shutter button and gently move your phone in that subject's direction. A creative blur will be used to capture the image.

Long exposure

Long Exposure is yet another Motion option that offers your pictures a unique appearance, much to Action Pan.

1. Launch the Pixel 9 or Pixel 9 pro's Camera app. in the first step
2. On the bottom bar, swipe twice to the right. You are now in motion mode

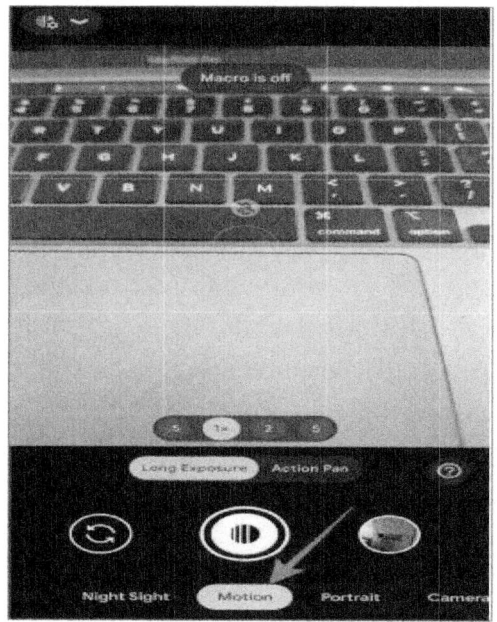

3. To change to the appropriate setting, click the Long Exposure option

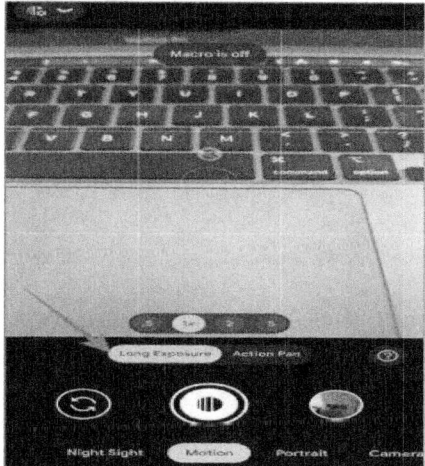

4. At this point, press the shutter button each time you notice a moving object. Hold your hands still until the picture is taken.

Astrophotography

1. Attach your Pixel 9 pro or Pixel 9 pro to a tripod or prop it up against a surface so it can remain still for a while. Be aware that you must complete this crucial step to use the Astrophotography mode.
2. On your Pixel 9 pro or Pixel 9 pro, open the Camera app
3. On the bottom bar, swipe three times to the right. You are now using Night Sight mode.

4. In the upper-left corner of the screen, tap the settings symbol.
5. Set Astrophotography to Auto after that

6. The shutter button will automatically activate if your phone is motionless.

Your Pixel 9 pro will begin taking pictures for a predetermined amount of time depending on the situation and the quantity of light available. Do not move the phone during this time since doing so will taint the result.

The picture will be taken when the countdown on the timer is complete. You may also view a brief timelapse of the motion of celestial bodies throughout that duration if you let the phone take pictures for more than 2.5 minutes.

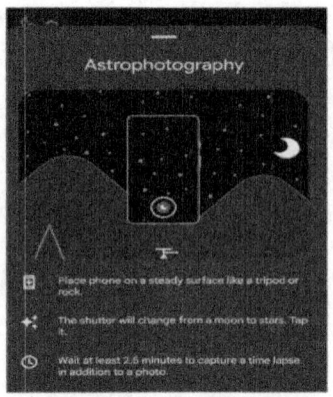

Setting Macro mode

1. Launch the Pixel 9 pro's Camera app.
2. Point the camera in the direction you wish to take a picture of. A macro toggle will instantly show up in the viewfinder

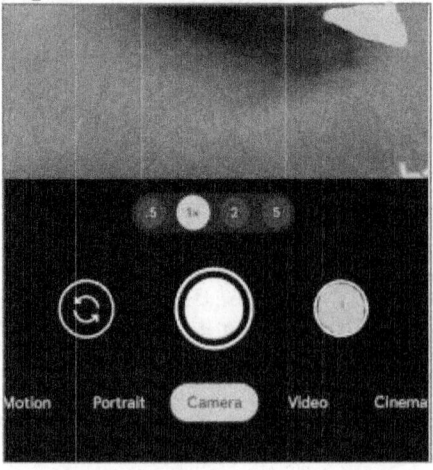

3. Tap the macro toggle to change to the appropriate lens. You may now get closer to the subject and take a macro picture.

Enhancing Speech

This is a need if you're taking videos outside in a loud setting. To activate Speech Enhancement, follow these steps.

1. Launch the Pixel 9 pro or Pixel 9 pro's Camera app.
2. Once on the bottom bar, swipe to the left. You are now in video mode

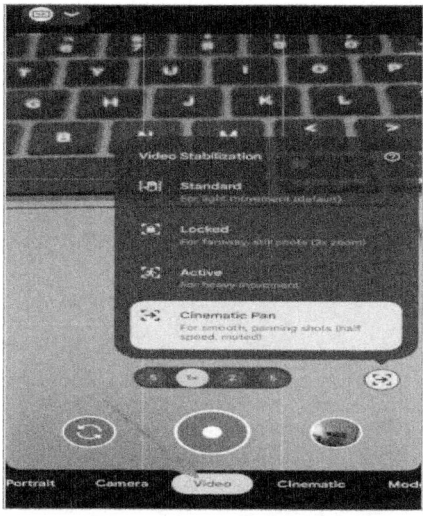

3. In the upper-left corner of the screen, tap the settings symbol.

4. Choose the video resolution of your choice. However, the function can only be used at 30 frames per second.

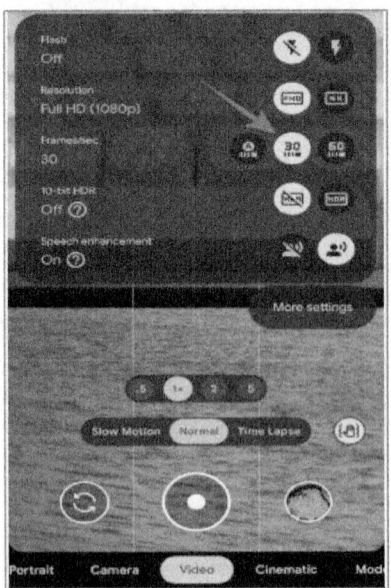

5. At this point, switch on Speech Enhancement.

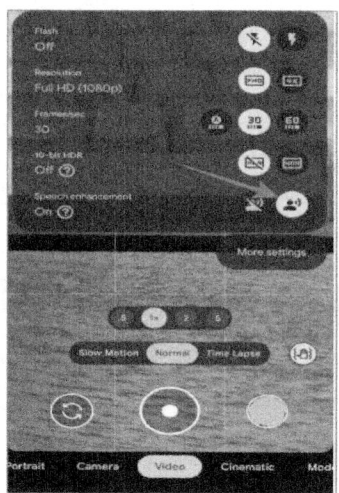

CHAPTER 12

Game mode

Turn on Game Mode

To use it, you don't need to download any additional software from a third party. Just follow the comprehensive instructions that follow.

1. The initial step is to launch the Settings app.
2. Go to Notifications right away

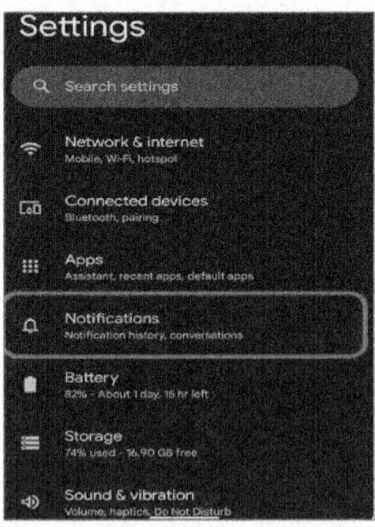

3. Navigate to the bottom and choose Do Not Disturb

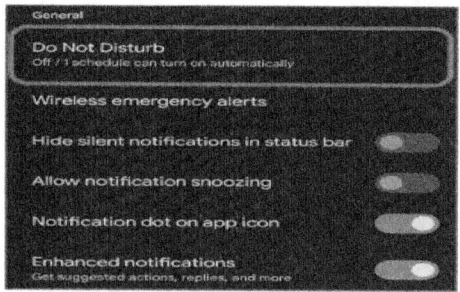

4. After that, click Schedules

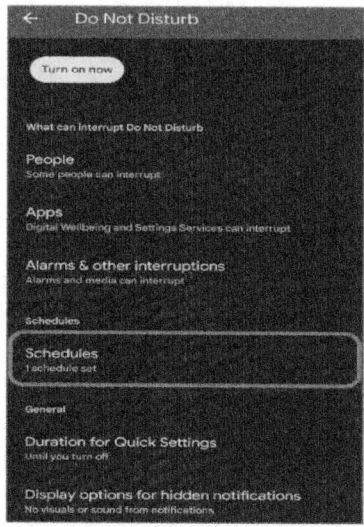

5. Next, choose the Gaming option and then click the gear button

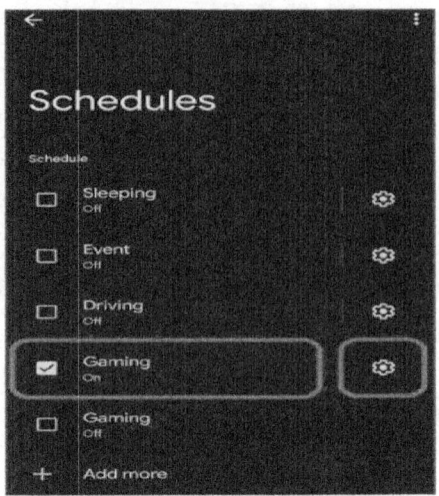

6. Turn on the Game Dashboard switch

You just need to do this to turn on Game Mode on your Google Pixel phone. When you turn on the option, each game you begin will display a little floating bubble on your screen. The floating game mode button may be moved by dragging it, and it can also be made invisible by dragging it off the screen.

- To access the Game Dashboard, tap the Game Mode bubble. You may choose to record gameplay, capture a snapshot, activate a frame rate counter, or enable Do Not Disturb. Below the aforementioned choices, there is a button for game optimization. It only applies to games that support Game Mode. Three modes will be offered to you in the option:

Use DND Mode to access the game's dashboard

1. Enter DND Mode by going to Settings > Notifications
2. then click the Game Mode phrase under Schedules
3. Simply turn on the toggle next to Game Mode at this point.

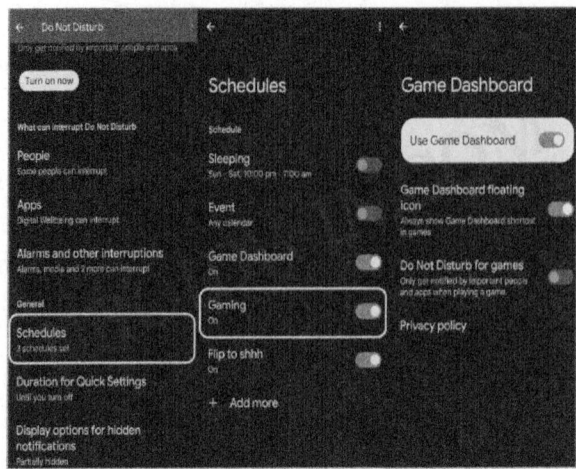

Access the Game Dashboard through the Google Page

Attempt to access it using the instructions provided below

1. Open the Game Dashboard by going to Settings > Google
2. Then just switch on the Game Mode option.

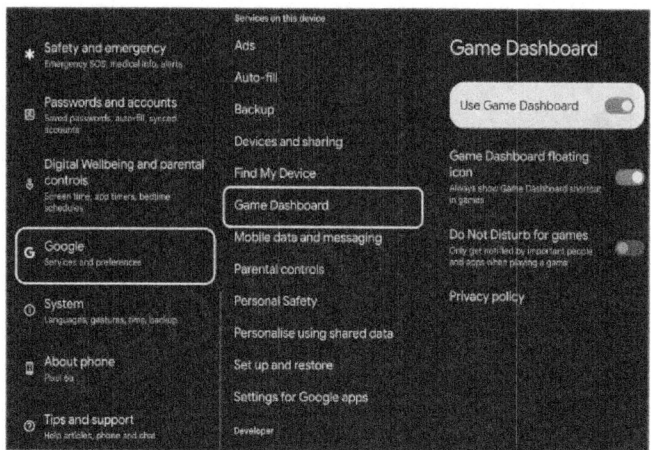

Change to English-only

Some customers found that the only method to enable Game Dashboard on their Pixel 9 pro was to switch the system language to English. So try this

- To access the languages and input menus, go to Settings > System.
- Then select Add a Language from the Languages menu.
- Via the displayed list, choose English, and then restart your device.

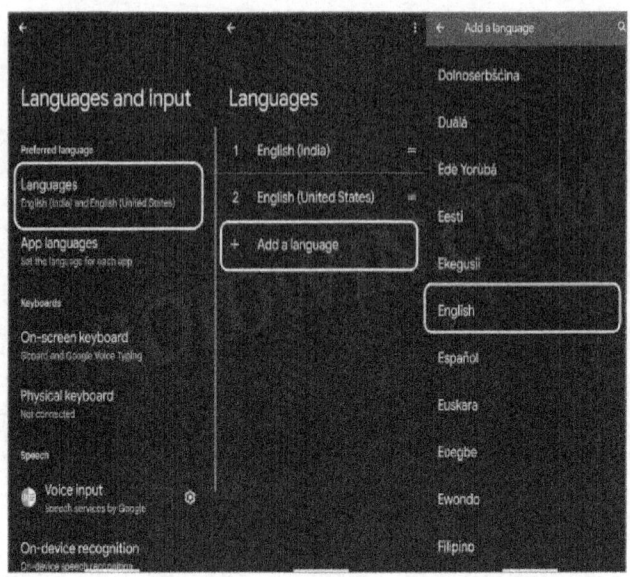

CHAPTER 13

How to Set Up contactless payment (NFC) on a Google Pixel 9

Activating NFC on your gadget

The smartphone's NFC module must first be turned on. Both the notification center and the device settings may be used for this.

Through the use of the notification center

Launch notification center via

1. Sliding downward via the upper section of the display screen
2. Hit on the NFC or contactless payment logo

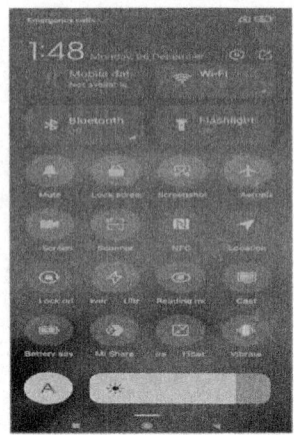

Utilizing the device's settings

Although less practical, this approach is nevertheless dependable. Take these easy steps:

1. Open your phone's settings.
2. Click on Connection and Sharing.
3. Activate the contactless payment (NFC) feature.

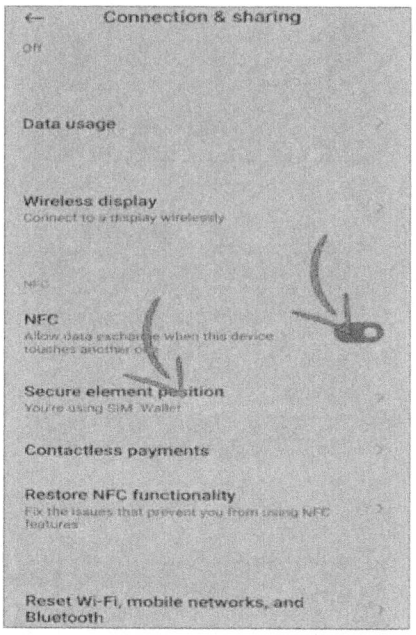

Since the "SIM Wallet" employs a chip within the SIM card for payment, it is also essential to put the "HCE Wallet" in the secure element position.

Setting up NFC

After turning on the module, you must set up NFC on the Google Pixel 9 pro by downloading a contactless payment app. Google Pay or the bank's app are two options. Let's see how to set up Google Pay for payments:

1. Launch the program
2. Click Start now

3. Add a Payment Method by tapping it

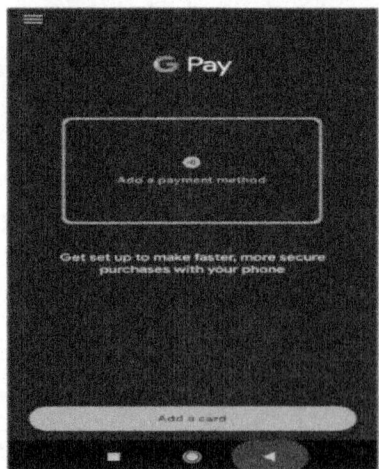

4. Select yourpayment method, credit card, or debit card.

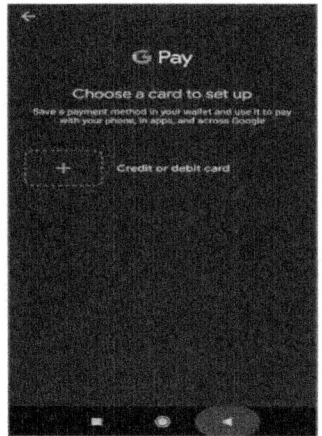

You must then enter the bank card's information, including the CVC code and card number. Then, you may use the Google Pixel 9 pro to pay for your purchases. However, it's firstly crucial to make sure Google Pay or another app you'll use for payments is set as your main. This step is necessary to configure NFC payment:

1. Open your phone's settings.
2. Please visit Contactless Payments
3. Choose Google Pay (or another app you intend to use) as the default payment method.

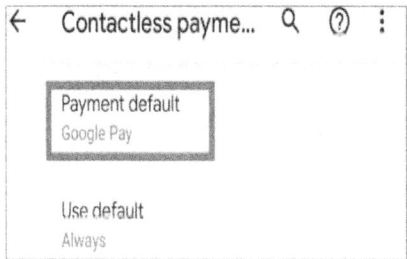

Remember that you can only do this with one payment app. You will have to manually activate the other application if you need to pay for a purchase using it.

CHAPTER 14

Emergency health and safety measures

How temperature is been measured

The temperature sensor on the Pixel 9 pro is conveniently located next to the camera and is simple to operate. It provides you with a temperature measurement by measuring the infrared radiation that the object emits. The sensor can detect temperatures as high as 392°F and as low as -4°F.

How to utilize the temperature-checking app Thermometer

Simply launch the Thermometer app that comes pre-installed on your Pixel 9 pro to utilize the temperature-measuring capability. You may use the search bar or the app drawer to locate it.

1. Launch the program, then select "Object temperature" Next, decide what kind of material the item you're measuring is made of

2. After that, press the "Tap to measure" button while holding your phone around two inches away from the object. For really little things, you might need to move a little bit closer.
    - Try measuring the portion of the object that isn't coated with hot steam if it is emanating from it, or wait to take the temperature until the steam has cleared. Consider it a photograph and make an effort to keep the steam out of your shot.

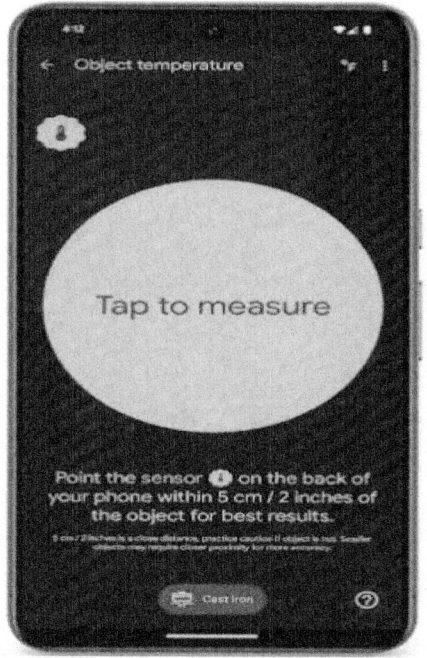

3. The temperature will show up on the screen in a few seconds. It's as simple as that.

Activate the Snore and Cough Detection

1. Using the App Drawer or Quick Settings on your Pixel 7, open the Settings app
2. Locate and choose the option labeled "Digital Wellbeing & Parental Controls."
3. You will then be able to navigate through the Bedtime Mode setups
4. Click the Cough and Snore Info tab in the Weekly Bedtime Summary. You'll be prompted to authorize access, so click OK to continue
5. This will bring up the necessary page where you may activate the snore and cough detection

Once you activate it, your phone will go into Bedtime Mode and it will begin to pick up on coughing and snoring.

Enable bedtime mode

1. Go to Settings
2. Select Digital Wellbeing & Parental settings by swiping up
3. Select "Bedtime mode."
4. Select Utilize a schedule under Bedtime Routine. Additional settings, such Turn on while charging, are included on the majority of supported phones. That will be helpful if you always charge your phone wirelessly or plug it in before going to bed or napping
5. Select a start and end time, if required
6. Decide which days you want Bedtime mode to activate on its own
7. To access further choices, tap Customize
8. The Do Not Disturb mode is initiated automatically. Touch the control switch to disable it.
9. Select Screen settings before going to bed to utilize backgrounds that are dimmed, dark, and grayscale
10. To toggle Bedtime mode on, hit on the Toggle-on icon.

Activate or deactivate earthquake alerts

note: You need to have data or Wi-Fi enabled to get notifications.

1. Activate your phone's Settings app.
2. Press the Safety & Emergency button. Earthquake notifications followed
3. Activate or deactivate earthquake alarms.

By default, earthquake notifications are activated. Only earthquakes in countries that are supported will cause you to receive warnings; you might not get alerts for every earthquake in your location. On rare occasions, you can receive an alert yet not experience an earthquake where you are.

CHAPTER 15

Car crashdetection

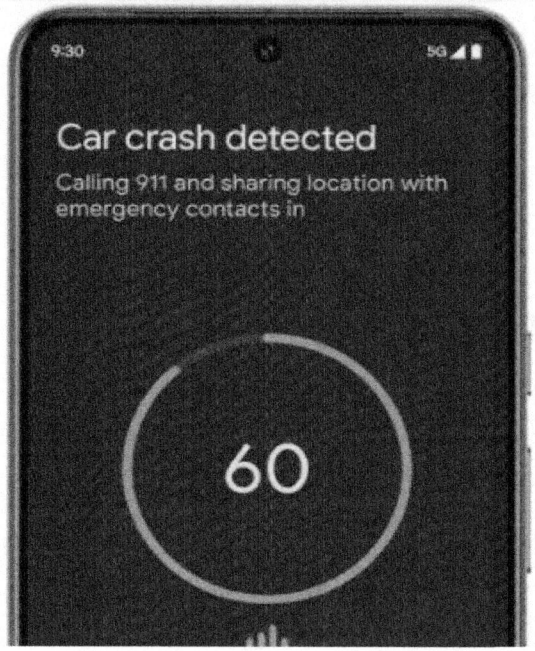

Set up car crashing detection
Your phone may automatically contact emergency agencies, such as 911 in the US, and disclose your position if it senses that you have been in a serious vehicular accident.

1. Launch the Personal Safety app on your phone
2. Select Features
3. Scroll down to "Car Crash Detection."
4. Select "Set up."

- While the app is running, hit Allow when prompted to disclose your location.
- Click Allow when prompted to share your microphone and movements.

Making use of your car crash detection

To become acquainted with the methodology for detecting auto crashes,

- Click On the Safety app's feature page,
- Try a demo before pressing Start.

Remember that this is only a simulation of the actions that the Pixel will take in case of an automobile collision.

- When your Pixel starts to vibrate and sound like a beacon, you will be given the option to either call 911 or swipe the I'm OK button.

In addition, if you are incapacitated and unable to interact with the Pixel, a countdown of sixty seconds will begin automatically, triggering the second choice.

- If you choose I'm OK, your Pixel will prompt you to either call 911 or label the detection as minor or no crash.
- Your position and its coordinates will be shared with a local dispatcher if you decide to dial 911.

Activate the car crash detection feature with emergency sharing.

1. Launch the Personal Safety app on your phone
2. Select Features at the bottom.
3. Select "Auto Crash Detection."
4. If your phone senses a crash, choose the emergency response option
   - Tap Emergency Sharing to SMS your position and updates to your emergency contacts.
   - When Car Crash Detection is activated, emergency agencies are automatically contacted.

If you react within 60 seconds of a crash being identified, you can:

- Press It's okay if I end the call
- Click Call 911 and let contacts know.

CHAPTER 16

Emergency/sos

Activate and configure Emergency SOS

These are the actions you need to take to finish this.

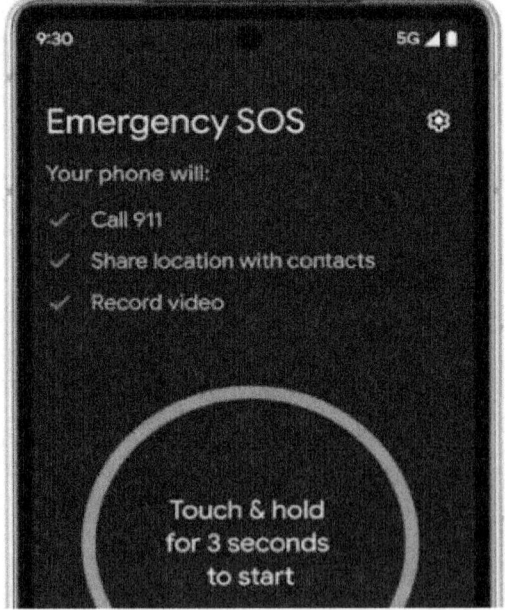

1. Activate your phone's Settings app.
2. Select Safety & Emergency, followed by Emergency SOS
3. Select "Start setup" at the bottom
4. Your phone can initiate emergency procedures if you need assistance

a. Tap Start to set up your emergency services number.
   - Tap Change number to modify the local emergency number if necessary
   - Press Next when you've determined the proper local number.
b. You can enable assisted calling on your phone to allow emergency personnel to know where you are if you are unable to reply.
   - To enable assisted calling, hit Turn on.
   - Advice: Assisted calling availability varies based on region.
c. Tap Start setup and then Set up to send updates and share your position with your emergency contacts.
   - Select a person to share information with an emergency by tapping Add contact.
   - Select the details you want Emergency SOS to provide to your emergency contact.
   - Press Next.
d. You have to give the Personal Safety app permission to access your location while you're using it to communicate your whereabouts in an emergency.

- Press Next, then when using the application.
e. Scroll down and choose Start Setup to have emergency SOS initiate an emergency recording while you continue to use the other capabilities of your phone.
    - To capture emergency footage, press Turn On, followed by when using the application.
    - After your video has been automatically backed up to your smartphone, you can select to share it with your emergency contacts. Select Next, then Share automatically after the backup
f. Select one of the following to initiate Emergency SOS actions:
    - Choose Press and Hold to initiate actions.
    - After the countdown, choose Start actions immediately. Turn on the Play alarm sound if you want this option to sound an alarm.
5. Select "Done."

Select how to begin Emergency SOS

Emergency SOS can be configured to initiate emergency activities automatically, or it can be configured to require a confirmation step before initiating any action.

1. Activate your phone's Settings app.
2. Select Safety & emergency and then press the SOS button
3. Select Settings from the "How it works" menu
4. There are two ways you may configure Emergency SOS:
   - To initiate an emergency action, press and hold the screen to add a confirmation step.
   - Tap Start activities automatically to initiate emergency steps automatically following a 5-second countdown.

Switch off the emergency SOS

1. Activate your phone's Settings app.
2. Select Safety & emergency and then press the SOS button
3. Select Settings from the "How it works" menu.
4. Press to disable the emergency SOS.

Utilize Emergency SOS to record video, notify contacts, and make an assistance request

1. Press the power button on your phone at least five times
2. To initiate the emergency call, tap and hold inside the red circle for three seconds, or wait for the countdown to begin automatically, depending on your settings
3. Depending on your settings, more emergency activities start when you initiate an emergency call.

Record video in an emergency

When things get serious, like informing your emergency contacts or contacting local agencies, emergency recording allows you to multitask.

With a bit rate of around 10MB per minute, it records video for up to 45 minutes.

- If **you enable auto-share**, a link to the video will be sent to your emergency contacts automatically unless you disable it within 15 seconds of the video being recorded.
- After each recording, if you enable auto-share, a link to your video will be sent to all of your emergency contacts automatically.

How automatic backup functions

To manage or organize your video content:

1. Launch the Personal Safety app on your phone
2. Select Your videos, followed by Your details
3. Select Share or Delete after tapping More next to a video.

Activate or deactivate Emergency Location Service

1. Activate your phone's Settings app.
2. Select Location and then select Google Emergency Location Service or Emergency Location Service under Location services
3. Activate or deactivate Google Emergency Location Service or Emergency Location Service.

Share and provide your emergency contacts with your location.

Launch the emergency sharing feature

1. Launch the Personal Safety app on your phone
2. Select "Emergency sharing."
3. Decide with whom you wish to share your current location in real-time.
    - A message will be optionally included
4. Select "Share."

5. To read the specifics of your Emergency sharing, tap the notice banner.

Quit sharing emergency information

1. Launch the Personal Safety app on your phone
2. Press the information about emergency sharing
3. Press the Stop button.
    - To clarify why you're ending the emergency sharing, you might provide a note.
    - Advice: After 24 hours, emergency sharing will automatically terminate.

CHAPTER 18

How to do a factory reset and enter safe mode

Safe Mode

Whenever the phone rings

1. Hit on and hold down the power knob
2. Touch and hold the symbol for powering off. You will be given the choice to restart in Safe Mode in a pop-up notification.
3. Tap OK.

In the absence of a phone or if the gadget is off

1. Hit on and hold down the power knob
2. Hold pressing the volume down button after the animation begins.
    - To start the phone in Safe Mode, keep holding it until the animation is finished.

Leave Safe Mode

1. Tap Restart after pressing the power button. The phone ought to immediately go back to regular mode
   - The power button may also be pressed and held down until the phone restarts.

Reset Factory settings

Reset the phone while it is powered on.
1. Navigate to settings System > Advanced, then hit on the reset option
2. Hit on erase every data and, then hit on reset phone
3. Input your pin code, and pattern, then hit on the erase everything

Reset the phone if it is off or unresponsive

1. Hit on and hold down the power & lower volume button simultaneously pending when Fastboot mode pops up
2. Hold down the power button as you push it if you see No command. Press the volume up button while still holding the power button, then let go of both
3. Make use of the volume keys to enter Recovery mode. Press the power button to pick an option.
4. You may select Wipe data/factory reset with the volume keys

5. Once the phone has been reset, choose Reboot system now.

CHAPTER 19

Common problems and issues

Do you have any issues with your Google Pixel 9 pro? In that case, ease up—you're not alone. We'll go through some of the most frequent issues with the Google Pixel 9 Pro

I'll demonstrate how to resolve bugs and issues on your Google Pixel 9 Pro

Poor or easily drained battery life

The steps listed below might be used if your Google Pixel 9 pro battery is fast depleting.

How to fix this

- At all times when GPS is not required, turn it off
- Uninstall any installed applications, such as phone cleaning. These background-running applications drain your phone's battery
- Download and install only apps from the Google Play store.

- These applications can be infected with malware that consumes your phone's battery in the background.
- Try to use your phone as often as possible in public. Avoid using your Google Pixel 9 pro in custom settings, as this may result in insufficient battery life
- Try replacing your battery if you notice a sharp decline in the power life of your phone
- High screen brightness settings on the Google Pixel 9 pro might cause your battery to drain quickly.This could also explain why your battery runs out quicker if you play more games.
- Examine whether your battery issues are related to the apps you have installed on your phone
- Uninstall any apps you may have installed that promise to increase your phone's battery life
- Long periods spent in power-saving mode on your phone also shorten its battery life
- Try a factory reset on your Google Pixel 9 pro if the battery issue persists after trying the aforementioned fixes.

Sluggish or laggy user interface

When using your phone, does the user interface feel slow and laggy? If so, then this is your device's comprehensive solution.

How to Reduce Lag on the Android Google Pixel 9 pro Device?

- Uninstall any antivirus or garbage-cleaning apps you may be running on your phone.
- Make sure there is enough room on your phone's internal storage. If your phone's storage is getting low, make some space available and your Google Pixel 9 pro phone will function normally again
- Connect your phone to a computer or laptop and run a Quick Heal or other reliable antivirus scan on it. The infection on your phone will be eliminated by it
- Due to slow connectivity, you could occasionally have a jerky and sluggish experience
- If the issue persists after doing the aforementioned procedures, attempt a factory reset on your phone
- Then choose "Erase all data (factory reset)" from the menu under Settings > System > Reset Options

- After a factory reset, there is a good chance that your phone will function considerably more quickly than it did before.
- Uninstalling useless applications is a good idea
- Occasionally, using a custom theme on your phone could cause it to run slowly.
- This issue could also have arisen because you just installed a third-party launcher on your Google Pixel 9 pro. You may remove it and go back to the stock theme.
- Try doing a simple reboot on your device to see if it resolves the issue
- Verify that your phone is running the most recent Android version. If not, you should update your phone to the most recent OS version.
- Once an update is available, update all of your apps.

Problems with your gadget's camera

It's unclear why the phone's camera keeps switching off at random. To correct it, simply follow the procedures listed below.

How Can the Pixel 9 pro Device's Camera Issues Be Fixed?

- Simply return to the default settings if you're experiencing difficulties with your camera settings.

- Image Stabilization should be enabled if you want to get the most out of your camera.
- If you're still having issues, try clearing the camera app's cache and launching it once again.
- For improved image quality, turn on the HD option in the camera app.
- Whether you have altered the camera settings in any way, go back to the original settings and see whether the issue has been resolved.
- Your phone's screen guard should be removed to see whether the problem is resolved.
- To address difficulties with blurry photos, you need also to clean the lens on your Google Pixel 9 pro.

Your gadget shutting down unexpectedly

Consider the instructions below if you experience the same issue with your Google Pixel 9 pro smartphone.

Solve unexpected shutdown?

1. First, make sure the battery in your Google Pixel 9 pro is functioning properly.
2. To do so, use the phone's dialer to dial *#*#4636#*#*.
    - It's now possible to see the "Battery information."
3. The unexpected shutdown of your phone might also be caused by the temperature of your phone, which may be rising rapidly

4. Avoid using heavy back coverings since poor airflow might lead to heating issues.
5. Check to see whether the internal storage on your phone has any free space. If not, this may be the cause of the sudden power outage.

Stuck or frozen Google Pixel 9 pro screen

The major reason for this problem on your Android phone is a lack of RAM. To address this problem, use the procedures listed below.

Fix the screen that is frozen or stuck.

First, check your smartphone for Android updates. Install any updates immediately if there is a new version.

1. If your phone has any applications that you do not use, remove them or force-stop them.
2. Safe-mode restart your Google Pixel 9 pro, then wait to see whether the issue resolves itself. If not, restart your phone normally and uninstall the offending app
3. When your phone's memory or storage is running low, you could occasionally have a frozen screen issue
4. If you encounter this problem when utilizing an app, then:
    - Click "Apps" and then "See All Apps" Clear the cache of the program you are having issues with.

- The Google Pixel 9 pro smartphone's factory reset is the final stage. Your issues could all be resolved by it.

Slow App Opening

You've probably seen several times that many programs open up quite slowly. If this problem occurs on your phone, use the easy procedures listed below.

How to Fix Apps Open Slowly?

1. Make sure your phone's internal storage has adequate room first. Delete some trash files and verify whether it's not
2. The poor RAM management on your phone is a common cause of this issue. You may then utilize the RAM Booster App. The general functionality of your gadget will be enhanced.
3. Verify your smartphone to see whether you have any modified apps or games loaded. Immediately remove it from the Google Pixel 9 pro if you have already done so.
4. You must restart your phone and verify if the issue is present in all of the apps. The possibility of success rises as a result.
5. Use the App's Lite version. It will cut down on RAM use and speed up app launching.
6. You should factory reset your phone if this issue persists.

Apps and Games Crash Suddenly or Unexpectedly

This is a typical problem that may be resolved by using the procedures listed below whenever you start an app or game and it abruptly closes.

Repair unexpected app crashes?

To start, navigate to Settings > Apps and look for the problematic app. For the chosen app, clear the data.

- Verify that there is at least 1 GB of storage available on your phone's internal storage.
- Reinstall the problematic software after uninstalling it first. It will prevent app crashes.
- Ensure that the program is downloaded in its most recent version.
- Make sure to disable Power Saving Mode or Safe Mode if you have them activated
- Finally, use an antivirus program to scan your device.

Bluetooth won't connect

When you activate Bluetooth and connect to other devices, is your Bluetooth disconnected?

Bluetooth connectivity problem be fixed?

- Check that your device is not running in safe mode.

- The OTA Updates may be the cause of this issue. Thus, check to see whether there is a new version available.
- Make careful to reset Bluetooth settings to default if you have made any modifications
- Verify whether other phones can locate your device.
- For a little while, turn off the Bluetooth on your phone, and then turn it back on
- Remove every device that was previously associated with the Google Pixel 9 pro, then see if the issue has been resolved.

Display broken&touch not functioning

The methods listed below should be followed if your Google Pixel 9 pro's display is damaged and you need to access your data.

How can data be accessed on a Google Pixel 9 pro if the touch screen isn't working?

- You may connect your Google Pixel 9 pro to your computer or laptop via a USB connection. By doing this, you can easily access all of your information.
- If you have data stored on your micro SD card, remove and reinsert it. See if this resolves the problem
- The screen sensor's malfunction may be the issue. Examine it and take necessary action.

- You may use an OTG cable to use any apps on your phone.
- Connect your wireless mouse and keyboard. You can now use your phone like a PC thanks to this.
- If your touch feature isn't working, try the methods above.

WiFi Connection Issue or LimitedWiFi Range

You can use the procedures listed below to fix the issue if your wifi connection is sluggish.

How can I fix the Google Pixel 9 pro's wifi connection issue?

1. The cause could occasionally be poor weather. When the weather is bad or wet
2. If there is a problem, you may reset your modem's settings or check it out
3. You might try repeatedly turning on and off the wifi router
4. Verify that you are not outside the range of the wifi router. It is the most frequent cause of low-range wifi.
5. Turn the Google Pixel 9 pro's Airplane Mode on for two to three minutes before turning it off. Verify if the problem has now been addressed.
6. Check to see whether you have reached your plan's bandwidth limit last.

Mobile data or cellular network issues

Try the following procedures if your phone network is fluctuating or you're not receiving a strong signal.

How can the Google Pixel 9 pro's troubles with cellular and mobile data networks be fixed?

- Remove the SIM card from your Google Pixel 9 pro handset, then replace it.
- If the issue persists, activate the airplane mode briefly before turning it off again
- You could try clearing the settings in your network
- Obstacles that stand between your phone and the cell tower are frequently the cause of this issue
- Check if the problem has been fixed by restarting your phone.
- Check to see whether a recently installed app is causing a network problem for you.

Applications from the Play Store won't download

You're not alone if you're experiencing problems downloading apps for your Google Pixel 9 pro from the Play Store. There are several potential causes for this problem, which many users have reported.

How to Fix the Google Pixel 9 pro's Play Store Apps Not Downloading Issue?

- Ensure that your Wi-Fi or mobile data connection is robust
- Verify the amount of storage space on your gadget.
- Try restarting your Google Pixel 9 pro smartphone to see if the problem has been resolved.
- Verify any system updates for Android
- Launch the Settings app
- Simply select System > Advanced > System upgrade
- Clear the Play Store's local search history next
- Try Google Play Store's Clear App Data. That issue with the app not downloading will be resolved.

Problem with the fingerprint scanner

A fingerprint scanner function on the Google Pixel 9 pro adds a degree of protection. However, we'll demonstrate how to solve the issue for you in this part.

How to Fix the Google Pixel 9 pro's Fingerprint Sensor Issue?

1. On a Google smartphone, there are several different ways to resolve issues with the fingerprint sensor.

2. Cleaning the sensor with a soft cloth or tissue is one potential remedy
3. Remove the registered fingerprint before adding a new one
4. You may also try upgrading the software on your Google Pixel 9 pro smartphone; new versions can provide remedies for any problems you might be having with the fingerprint sensor
5. Reinstalling the software linked to your device's biometric capabilities is an additional choice that might occasionally assist in resolving any difficulties with the fingerprint sensor.
6. In the end, you might need to speak with Google customer service to figure out and fix any unique issues you might be having with the fingerprint sensor on your smartphone.

Your gadget heatingissue

This is a typical problem that can be fixed with a few adjustments.

How can the heating issue be fixed?
- Unplug the phone after it has finished charging entirely. It frequently results in overheating issues.
- Use a thin back cover, please. Using a thick back cover might prevent your phone from being properly ventilated and result in heating issues

- Avoid using your phone excessively while it is charging and refrain from playing games while it is charging
- Whenever charging the Google Pixel 9 pro smartphone, always use the original charger
- Installing unsupported apps and games on your phone is not advised. It frequently results in overheating issues
- Always keep your phone up to date, and update all of your applications frequently
- Never allow the storage on your phone to fill up. This might cause your phone to become slow and have heating issues.
- Even heating issues might occasionally occur due to the warm climate in your house
- Download your applications only from the Google Play Store. The Internet-downloaded programs might occasionally lead to heating issues
- The primary cause of the Google Pixel 9 pro smartphone overheating is a battery that is too old and in poor condition.

BONUS TIPS

Whats New in the Google Pixel 9 series

Screenshot app

1. Navigate to the screenshot app on your device's home screen
2. Scroll through it to access and see your screenshots
3. Utilize the search or find bar to input & search your stored screenshots

Pixel-Studio

Pixel Studio serves as an artistic canvas for you. A picture generator unlike any other is Pixel Studio. With your phone, you can now create anything from the ground up—it's a real creative canvas.

It is powered by a combination of cloud-based Image 3 text-to-image model and an on-device diffusion model running on Tensor G4.

An improved weather app

The Pixel Weather app now has an exquisite look and exceptionally precise weather predictions. To give you an idea of the day's weather, Gemini Nano will also provide a personalized AI weather report.

Magic Editor's Reimagine feature makes editing simpler

- Just write anything you want in a text field and use Magic Editor's Reimagine feature to watch your thoughts come to life.
- Use your imagination to alter the appearance of inside décor, grass, sky, trees, and other elements in your pictures

Using a circle to search updated features

Google can be used to search everything you discover on your Pixel phone or tablet without requiring you to open another app.

1. To be able to redo this Circle to Search, slide upward via the screen's display lower section
2. Launch the YouTube application
3. Touch and hold the bottom navigation bar of your screen when viewing a YouTube short or any other kind of video
4. A search box for Google will show up.

To search a specific area of the image, circle it.

As an additional option, you can tap or draw over the area you wish to search

5. The lower section of your display will pop up your search result
6. Swipe down or hit the Close button in the upper left corner of the screen when you're finished and want to go back to the original app context

Deactivate the circle to search

Via the three-button navigation mode:

1. Go to Settings & open it
2. Find the Circle to search
3. Click on the Circle to search
4. Switch the Circle to Search off.

With Additional camera upgrades to provide breathtaking images and movies & other features, you will learn from this manual

INDEX

A

Access and modify navigation bar settings, 50
Access and modify Quick Settings and notifications, 47
Access and use screen recording, 92
Access and utilize Google Lens, 109
Access Night Sight and utilize it, 107
Access the camera and microphone for editing, 90
Access the camera's modes, 97
Access the Game Dashboard through the Google Page, 132
Access/open/close browser tabs, 64
Accessing and Archiving Your Photos and Videos, 87
Accessing your browser setup, 65
Accessing your cellular data, 57
Accessing your device's split screen, 81
Action Pan, 119
Activate and configure Emergency SOS, 150
Activate or deactivate earthquake alerts, 146
Activate or deactivate Emergency Location Service, 155
Activate or deactivate mobile data, 58
Activate or deactivate the shutter sound, 98
Activate the car crash detection feature with emergency sharing, 149
Activate the Macro mode, 106
Activate the Snore and Cough Detection, 144
Activate/deactivate gestures, 48
Activate/deactivate mobile hotspot, 69
Activating Fast Charging, 18
Activating NFC on your gadget, 135
Activating Wireless Charging, 20
Active Stabilization, 117
Add a second SIM card & eSIM, 44
Adjust or modify your photo's size, 88
Adjust the camera's focus, 105
Advanced Photos & Videos, 97
An improved weather app, 174
Applications from the Play Store won't download, 170
Apps and Games Crash Suddenly or Unexpectedly, 167
Astrophotography, 122

B

Battery Adaptive and Charging, 21
Bluetooth, 73
Bluetooth won't connect, 167
BONUS TIPS, 174
Bookmark website, 63
Browsing the Internet (web), 62

C

Camera and Video Presets, 87
camera settings on your gadget, 87
Car crash detection, 147
Change to English-only, 133
Charging your gadget, 17
Check your network connection's strength, 56
Cinematic Mode, 114
Cinematic Pan, 115
circle to search updated, 175
Common problems and issues, 160
Connecting to a secret network, 68
Connectivity, 73
Create a video or take pictures, 104
Crop a picture, 98
Customize photo and video settings, 97

D

Deactivate the circle to search, 176
Device Security and safety, 23
disable Face Unlock, 27
Display broken & touch not functioning, 168

E

easily drained battery life, 160
Edit a Screenshot, 91
Emergency health and safety measures, 141
Emergency/sos, 150
Enable bedtime mode, 145
End recording, 93
Enhancing Speech, 125

F

Fingerprint Setup, 29
Forget a Network service, 67

G

gadget heating issue, 172
gadget shutting down unexpectedly, 164
Game mode, 128
Go to website, 62

H

hotspot tethering in sharing connection, 74
How automatic backup functions, 155
How to charge your Pixel, 17
How to do a factory reset and enter safe mode, 157
How to Set Up contactless payment (NFC), 135

I

Inserting a SIM card into your gadget, 43
Internet and Cellular Info, 56
Introduction, 1

J

Join a wireless network (wifi), 66

L

Leave Safe Mode, 158
Leave the Split Screen, 84
Live Translate, 76
Long exposure, 120

M

Magic Editor's Reimagine feature makes editing simpler, 175
Make use of WiFi, 66
Making use of your car crash detection, 148
Media transfer to or via a PC, 94
Mobile (portable) Hotspot, 69
Mobile data or cellular network issues, 170
Modify the window's size, 83
Motion & Gestures, 47
Multitask with your device, 79

O

On/Off the flash switch, 89
Open two applications at once, 79

P

Photos and Videos, 87
Physical characteristics, 4
Pixel-Studio, 174
Place a timer, 89

Problem with the fingerprint scanner, 171
Problems with your gadget's camera, 163

Q

Quit sharing emergency information, 156

R

Reconfigure the power button, 10
Record a Video, 110
Record video in an emergency, 154
Recording or Making a video, 110
Reset Factory settings, 158
Reset the phone if it is off or unresponsive, 158
Restart or turn off your Google Pixel, 7

S

Safe Mode, 157
screen lock and pattern, 33
Screenshot app, 174
Secure your phone using a pattern and pin, 33
Select how to begin Emergency SOS, 153
Set up car crashing detection, 147
Set up the Mobile Hotspot settings, 71
Setting Macro mode, 124
Setting up Face Unlock, 23
Setting up NFC, 137

Setup (Configure) your new Device, 12
Share a Screenshot, 91
Share and provide your emergency contacts with your location, 155
SIM AND e-SIM, 41
Slow App Opening, 166
Sluggish or laggy user interface, 162
smart lock, 32
Snap a still picture while in video mode, 111
Snapping a screenshot, 91
Start recording, 92
Stop, pause, and resume a recording, 111
Stuck or frozen Google Pixel 9 pro screen, 165
Summary of Google pixel, 3
Super-res Zoom, 114
Swapping between the front-facing and rear-facing cameras, 104
Switch Bluetooth On & off Using the Settings app, 73
Switch Bluetooth on or off via quick settings, 73
Switch off the emergency SOS, 153
Switch SIMs when making calls, 45
Switch your gadget on, 6

T

Take a picture, 104
Tethering via USB cable, 74
To pause the video, 111

Toggle on or off mobile data quickly, 60
Toggle your gadget off, 7
Transfer files via your device, 75
Transfer your videos and photos, 94
Transferring files to or via Macs, 95
Translate a discussion into a foreign language using Google Assistant, 78
Translate using the camera, 77
Turn a SIM off momentarily, 46
Turn on Game Mode, 128
Turn on Live Translation, 76
two SIM cards, 44

U

Use and access Panorama, 108
Use and access Picture Sphere, 108
Use Bluetooth to tether, 74
Use DND Mode to access the game's dashboard, 131
Use extra applications, 48
Use Google Assistant to toggle off your gadget, 9
Use Live Captioning when watching media in any language, 78
Use motions gestures for the full-screen, 51
Use photo effects, 103
Using a magic eraser, 99
Using an app to launch in a pop-up window, 80
Using Live Translation on Text Messages, 77

180

Using Picture-in-Picture, 85
Using split-screen modes, 79
Utilise flip to mute, 54
Utilize a button to toggle off the power, 9
Utilize Emergency SOS to record video, notify contacts, and make an assistance request, 154
Utilize filters, 99
Utilize Night Vision, 102
Utilize Photo Un-blur, 101
Utilize Quick Tap, 54
Utilize Slow Motion, 112
Utilize the Motion mode, 102
utilize the temperature-checking app Thermometer, 141
Utilize Time Lapse, 113
Utilizing the device's settings, 136

W

WiFi Connection Issue or Limited WiFi Range, 169
WiFi/hotspot settings &usage, 66
Wireless charging, 20
Wireless data transfer, 75

Z

Zoom in and out, 105

Printed in Great Britain
by Amazon